FDR's AMERICA

FDR's AMERICA

David E. Kyvig

University of Akron

FORUM PRESS

First Printing March 1976
Second Printing March 1977

Published simultaneously in Canada

Printed in the United States of America

Library of Congress Catalog Card Number: 75-44702

ISBN: 0-88273-201-3

Cover Design by Bruce Armstrong

Contents

To Jennifer and Elizabeth

Preface

More than 40 years after Roosevelt's inauguration and 30 years after World War II, we are still trying to understand and adjust to forces set in motion between 1933 and 1945. *FDR's America* probes into these and other significant aspects of that turbulent age through a series of fascinating, hitherto unpublished insights by participants in great or small events of the period. The New Deal and World War II are treated as equally significant, intertwined aspects of the Roosevelt years. The book is designed to stimulate interest in a variety of issues and events, and its chapters can be used in various combinations to focus on national politics, social life, minorities, agriculture, or labor and business. *FDR's America* may either complement a text in U.S. history survey courses or be used with the readings in a twentieth century American history course.

Participant memoirs, accounts by witnesses involved in the events they describe, form the core of *FDR's America*. Six accounts are contemporary diary entries, speeches, reports, radio broadcasts, or testimony before Congress. The other five were recorded after Roosevelt's death. Three were college lectures to undergraduate audiences and two were based on interviews. These memoirs represent the opinions of high government officials, the attitudes of government critics and the views of persons carrying on their own affairs during a turbulent era. The accounts reflect the experiences of farmers and workers, northerners and southerners, blacks and whites, men and women, elites and common folk. Each reveals an important facet of the New Deal or World War II, and together they present a meaningful picture of a complex age.

A historian with a special interest in the particular topic edited and introduced each chapter. The introductions describe the background of the author or authors of the accounts and place the account in a larger perspective. To assist the reader, each introduction contains several provocative questions pertinent to the particular account. The language of the original accounts remains for the most part untouched in the belief that, while not always graceful or grammatically correct, it invariably offers rich glimpses of human personality. An introductory chronological overview of the period and a brief analytical conclusion provide a framework for the reader. A list of suggested readings designed for the beginning scholar is included and concentrates on books available in paperback or obtainable at most libraries.

Many individuals and institutions assisted in the preparation of this book. I am pleased to acknowledge their generous support and express my appreciation to them.

Permission to use various participant memoirs was granted by Kalamazoo College, sponsor of the James Farley, Rexford Tugwell, and Adolf Berle lectures; the Iowa State Historical Department, Division of the State Historical Society; the Eleutherian Mills Historical Library; the Louisiana State University Library, Department of Archives and Manuscripts; the University of Akron American History Research Center; the United Rubber Workers; Daniel L. Powers; Lillian Powers Gonder; and Roland A. White.

Photographs were obtained from and appear with the permission of the National Archives, the Library of Congress Prints and Photographs Division, the United States Army Signal Corps, the United Rubber Workers, United Press International and the Iowa State University Press.

Scholars who read the manuscript and suggested improvements include George Knepper, University of Akron; Franklin Mitchell, University of Southern California; Peter Tyor, Illinois Institute of Technology; Neal Brooks, Essex Community College; Howard Ellis, Lorain Community College; Ken Weatherbie, Del Mar College; Robert Seifert, University of Virginia and University of Akron graduate students Richard Shrake and Willard Thomas.

I express my appreciation to the typists who prepared the manuscript: Maggie Burnes, Garnette Dorsey, Linda Foley, Patricia Godfrey, Pamela Lagodich, Elizabeth Siegel and Pamela Weiss.

My wife, Barbara, provided encouragement, and my daughters, Jennifer and Elizabeth, to whom this volume is dedicated, gave me just enough peace and quiet to finish the manuscript.

Finally the historians who contributed chapters were extraordinarily cooperative. They assumed tasks, met deadlines, and accepted editorial revisions with good grace. Their advice improved the manuscript. The merits of this volume are largely due to their efforts. As for the book's defects, I accept all responsibility.

Akron, Ohio   *David E. Kyvig*

*Franklin Roosevelt waving at the crowd during his inaugural
parade, March 4, 1933. [Marine Corps Photo National Archives]*

Introduction

Late Thursday afternoon, April 12, 1945, radio stations throughout America interrupted their programs to broadcast the news that Franklin Delano Roosevelt, thirty-second President of the United States, had died of a cerebral hemorrhage. The news shocked millions of Americans. Many were frightened, not only by the thought of having to confront the uncertainties of a postwar world led by a little-known U.S. Senator from Missouri, Harry S Truman, who had been elevated to the vice presidency only three months earlier, but also by the simple prospect of a government not headed by FDR. Many Americans reaching adulthood had never been conscious of any president other than Franklin Roosevelt; he had occupied the White House for more than twelve years. Furthermore, Roosevelt served during two of the nation's greatest crises: the Great Depression of the 1930s and the Second World War. The nation would survive the loss of its only four-time-elected president, of course, but countless persons would never be able to separate the man from the events of those dozen years. For millions, the era of the depression and World War II would always be the age of Franklin D. Roosevelt.

The age, of course, belonged not only to Roosevelt. It belonged to everyone who struggled through those years of economic chaos and bloodshed, occasional happiness but frequent misery. Roosevelt as an active, vocal national leader served as a focal point for well over a decade, but the president could not reflect all the attitudes nor share all the experiences of his fellow citizens. To understand the history of the New Deal and World War II, it is necessary to appreciate the role of Franklin Roosevelt, but it is equally important to consider the perspective of his critics and the experiences of average people merely seeking to survive those troubled times.

This volume seeks to examine the New Deal and World War II through the eyes of a number of people of varied backgrounds and concerns who lived through those years. Some of them, like James Farley, Rexford Tugwell, and Adolf Berle, were friends and associates of the president. Others, such as Milo Reno, Jouett Shouse, and Fulton Lewis, Jr., were severe critics. Still others, like Rex Murray, Elmer Powers, Walter White, and Mary Anderson, were less interested in the man in the White House than in the problems of their own particular social or economic group. Each person whose account forms a part of this collection watched events unfold from a different vantage point, and therefore each drew different conclusions. The fact that some of their observations were recorded in the midst of the period while others were set down years later after long reflection also contributes to the variety of perspectives. Taken together, these accounts by no means provide a comprehensive view of the period, but they do suggest the great complexity of social, political, and economic developments and the rich variety of human experiences which took place between 1933 and 1945. Furthermore, the accounts and the introductions to them by various historians suggest that much remains to be learned about the New Deal and the war. Not only do gaps in knowledge exist, but the meaning of many developments is open to dispute. These first-hand accounts are intended to provide information and to stimulate the reader to explore and ponder. Before examining them, it may be useful to consider briefly some major events and trends of the era.

When Franklin Roosevelt took the presidential oath on March 4, 1933, he assumed leadership of a nation confronting an unparalleled economic crisis. For more than three years the economy had been crumbling. The stock market crash of 1929; the disintegration of business and consumer confidence; the decay of an overextended credit system; the increasingly sharp decline of production, wages, and employment; and by the winter of 1932, the collapse of the banking system provided successive signs of the steadily worsening situation. Human misery multiplied as the economy slid downward, as the resources of municipal and state agencies as well as private charity were exhausted, and as the federal government failed to intervene. President Herbert Hoover, a humane and energetic man who believed deeply in the ability of private individuals and groups working cooperatively to restore the economy to health, feared that emergency federal relief programs would become permanent bureaucracies, undermining individual self-reliance and the free enterprise system. Finally forced into action by the desperate state of the economy, Hoover late in 1931 recommended creation of the Reconstruction Finance Corporation, a federal agency which Congress quickly empowered to loan $2 billion to endangered businesses and financial institutions. The Hoover administration thereby became the first to directly intervene in a peacetime economy. This action proved too little and too late to prevent further decline. By the winter of 1933 as many as 14 million workers — fully one quarter of the labor force — were unemployed. Hoover, preparing to leave office after repudiation at the polls, confessed, "We are at the end of our string."

Franklin Roosevelt, the man who carried 42 states to Hoover's six in the November, 1932, election, won largely because of public hostility to the Republican incumbent. Roosevelt himself offered no clear plan for economic recovery. The only son of an aristocratic Hudson River Valley family, FDR had led a pampered childhood, attended the best private schools (Groton, Harvard, Columbia Law), and married his fifth cousin Eleanor in the society wedding of 1905. His upbringing gave Roosevelt enormous self-confidence in dealing with all varieties of people and problems. He almost always seemed cheerful, or, if the occasion was somber, assured and optimistic. In his first try for political office in 1910, he won a seat in the New York state senate. FDR built a reputation as a reformer and became an early supporter of Woodrow Wilson. With Wilson's election as president in 1912, Roosevelt moved to Washington where he spent eight years as Assistant Secretary of the Navy — the same post from which distant cousin Theodore Roosevelt had launched his national political career. In 1920 the 38 year-old Roosevelt became the Democratic vice-presidential nominee on a ticket with James Cox and gained widespread recognition and acclaim despite a landslide loss to

Warren Harding and Calvin Coolidge. FDR's apparently bright future suddenly was endangered when he contracted polio in 1921. After achieving partial rehabilitation, Roosevelt was elected governor of New York in 1928, winning by a narrow margin. Four years of experience with the problems of depression in the largest state; liberal positions on issues of public utilities, conservation, agriculture, and unemployment relief; an overwhelming reelection victory in 1930; and an aggressive campaign for the nomination made Governor Roosevelt the Democratic candidate for president in 1932.

In his speech accepting the presidential nomination, FDR promised, if elected, a "new deal" for the American people. However vague, the label stuck. The Roosevelt administration immediately created an image of optimism, energy and action in sharp contrast to the departed Hoover government. "The New Deal" seemed to many an appropriate description of the change. But how "new" was the New Deal, and what exactly did that catchy phrase represent? In the first account in this collection (chapter one), former Democratic National Chairman James A. Farley implies that the personality of Franklin Roosevelt formed the core of the New Deal and that FDR was as conservative as he was cheerful, that he restored confidence and provided effective leadership without departing from traditional American principles.

Upon taking office, Roosevelt confronted a true emergency as well as the general problem of depression. Beginning in mid-February, 1933, states declared bank holidays, closing all banks, to forestall panic withdrawals which threatened collapse of the banking system. By March 4 the nation's banks had ceased to function. The new president quickly called a special session of Congress to propose legislation for currency expansion, federal examination of banks and the reopening of sound institutions. Congress approved it within hours. Soon most banks opened, people began to redeposit hastily withdrawn savings, and the banking crisis ended. Most observers admired the prompt restorative action. But some, recognizing that a private capitalistic banking system had been saved when even some bankers had been willing to accept government operation of the nation's financial institutions, found Roosevelt's solution quite conservative. During the balance of "The Hundred Days," as the three-month special session became known, the Roosevelt program seemed a strange mixture of radical change and conservatism.

The Hundred Days session saw a tremendous outpouring of significant legislation. Some, such as the Tennessee Valley Authority (TVA) Act creating a federal agency for regional development, flood control, and electric power production, the Federal Emergency Relief Act providing $500 million in federal funds for direct relief to the unemployed, and the Federal Deposit Insurance Corporation (FDIC) legislation to insure bank-savings accounts, had long been discussed by Congress and needed only an approving nod from FDR. Other ideas, such as the Civilian Conservation Corps (CCC), a program for putting 250,000 unemployed men to work under army supervision in national forests, and the Home Owner's Loan Corporation, a plan of government assistance to mortgage holders, came from the White House. Two of the most significant acts reflected compromises between Congress and the executive. The Agricultural Adjustment Act (AAA), an effort to aid desperate farmers, combined the administration's domestic allotment program (a plan involving price subsidies and production reduction paid for by taxing processors of agricultural commodities) with congressional proposals for currency inflation (to reduce the burden of mortgages on persons deeply in debt). The National Industrial Recovery Act sought to accommodate proponents of government economic planning, business self-regulation, and greater power for workers. The act allowed an industrial trade association to prepare a code of fair practices, free from anti-trust restrictions, so that industry-wide production planning would occur. The National Recovery Administration (NRA) would help draft and would administer the codes. Congress, in section 7(a) of the act, stipulated that codes must include minimum wage and maximum hours provisions and for the first time guaranteed labor the right to collective bargaining.

Contradictions loomed large in the Hundred Days. An "Economy Act" to balance the budget by reducing federal salaries and veterans benefits was soon followed by major new spending programs to stimulate recovery. Legislation for federal supervision of banking, the stock market, and railroads was passed as was the NRA program of business self-regulation. Measures assuming federal responsibility for the unemployed and ailing sectors of the economy and for monetary, fiscal, and production manipulation accompanied efforts to revive and restore private enterprise. The unifying theme of the early New Deal was not coherent planning but action. Roosevelt was an experimentalist who argued, "It is common sense to take a method and try it. If it fails, admit it frankly and try another. But above all, try something." Some condemn FDR as an opportunist and the New Deal as an effort to provide something for everyone no matter how inconsistent. But Rexford G. Tugwell, for several years a member of Roosevelt's inner circle, suggests in his account (chapter two) that the programs of the Hundred Days formed a sensible response to the depression and lifted the nation's hopes.

During the balance of 1933 and 1934, little was added to the legislative package of the Hundred Days. The thrust of government activity was to implement the AAA, NRA, and other programs. The gloom which had settled over American society seemed to recede a bit. Roosevelt's image of energetic leadership, his reassuring frequent radio broadcasts, and the relief provided by various New Deal programs all contributed. Young men flocked to the CCC. Federally-funded relief projects provided more jobs. TVA provided cheap electric power, fertilizer, and flood control to farmers in much of the South. Unemployment fell by more than two million. The public mood improved, and the Democrats won a ringing endorsement in the 1934 congressional elections. Yet the basic economic depression remained. National income for 1934 was about half of what it had been in 1929, and nearly ten million workers — one in five — were still out of work.

Under the circumstances, some understandably became disenchanted with the New Deal. Displeasure was voiced by those who thought the Roosevelt administration had done too little. American agriculture had experienced depression since the end of World War I, and some farmers regarded the AAA as a wrongheaded and feeble attempt to solve their problems. Farm leader Milo Reno's 1934 account (chapter three) clearly displays this sentiment. Reno's theme was repeated with variations by several other vocal individuals with sizeable followings. Senator Huey Long of Louisiana argued that the New Deal was too timid and business-oriented. What was needed, said Long, was to "share the wealth", confiscate large incomes and estates through heavy graduated taxes and redistribute these funds so that all would have a decent minimum income. More money would be put in the hands of those likely to consume and stimulate production. A retired medical doctor, Francis Townsend of California, called for relief to the elderly and economic stimulation through $200 a month government pensions which would have to be spent immediately. Father Charles Coughlin of Detroit, a Catholic priest with a weekly nationwide radio audience in the tens of millions, offered a program of centralized economic planning and control together with social welfare which some felt resembled National Socialism of Hitler's Germany.

At least as unhappy were many businessmen who felt that the New Deal not only had failed to solve the riddle of depression but had dangerously expanded the power of the federal government in efforts to do so. A group of them founded the American Liberty League in 1934. Some disliked government regulation and supervision of business activities while others clearly feared that growing federal expenditures would lead to sharply increased taxation of large incomes. A genuine worry that chaos would result if traditional patterns of government were abandoned was intertwined with clear-cut economic self-interest. These concerns about the New Deal abound in Liberty League President Jouett Shouse's 1935 account (chapter four).

Growing discontent on both the left and right, together with Supreme Court action declaring the AAA and NRA unconstitutional and the realization that the Hundred Days legislation had not ended the depression, moved the Roosevelt administration to undertake a new program of reform and recovery in 1935 and 1936. This flurry of activity appeared so distinctive from what had preceded it that some historians have labeled it a "second New Deal." A new emphasis was placed on direct federal intervention in the economy to assure the welfare of the individual. Among the measures adopted were the Social Security Act, a program of old age pensions and unemployment compensation financed by taxes on workers' wages and employers' payrolls; the Banking Act of 1935, which expanded federal control over the banking system; a new $5 billion relief program called the Work Projects Administration (WPA) to provide work for the unemployed; and the Wealth Tax Act which modestly increased taxes on high incomes. This legislation further outraged conservatives but mollified some liberal and radical critics.

One of the most notable measures of the second New Deal was the National Labor Relations Act, often called the Wagner act after its principal author, Democratic Senator Robert Wagner of New York. The NRA provisions regarding unionization proved inadequate. Wagner therefore proposed creation of a permanent independent agency to assure the rights of workers to bargain collectively. The National Labor Relations Board (NLRB) would supervise union elections, compel employers to bargain with unions, and restrain business from committing unfair labor practices against unions or their members. Initially the Roosevelt administration failed to support Wagner. But after the Supreme Court's destruction of the NRA, FDR called the bill "must legislation," and it was quickly passed. Labor leader Rex Murray's account (chapter five) of efforts to win union demands in the rubber industry vividly describes the difficulties facing workers before adoption of the Wagner act. Creation of the NLRB did not solve all problems as revealed in the account (chapter five) of Mrs. Sherman Dalrymple, wife of a union official. Sit-downs and strikes in the automobile, steel, and rubber industries and elsewhere would be required before employers signed union contracts. Yet federal support for the rights of workers to join unions proved to be one of the major innovations of the decade.

The second New Deal also affected farmers. The Supreme Court in January 1936, declared unconstitutional the tax on processors of agricultural products, a key provision of the AAA which funded the payments to farmers for reducing crop and livestock production. Rather than abandon the concept of production restriction to raise farm prices, FDR proposed the Soil Conservation and Domestic Allotment Act which paid farmers from general tax revenues to plant soil-enriching grasses and legumes rather than cash crops. Iowa farmer Elmer Powers in his diary for 1937 (chapter six) indicates this was both a financial help and a bureaucratic headache. Powers implies that another act of the second New Deal was more important to farmers. The Rural Electrification Administration (REA), created in May 1935, provided loans to erect power lines throughout the countryside. At the time only one out of ten farms, mainly in the northeast and midwest, received electricity. By 1941 four out of ten farms were electrified; by 1950, nine out of ten. Electric power allowed farmers to enjoy modern appliances, to ease their work load while expanding their output, to share broadcasts of news and entertainment, in short, to live more like residents of urban America.

The second phase of the New Deal, though considerably more advanced than the first, also mixed innovation and conservatism. In the Social Security Act, the National Labor Relations Act, the REA, and the Soil Conservation and Domestic Allotment Act, the federal government directly assisted individuals confronted by economic forces beyond their control. Yet the Social Security Act did not completely assume government responsibility for the aged and unemployed. Social Security was funded by taxes on individual earnings rather than from general federal revenues; workers themselves, rather than the society as a whole, carried the burden. Furthermore, benefits were paid in proportion to earnings rather than need, and many workers, including some of the most needy such as domestic servants and farm laborers, were not covered at all. Compared to other national welfare systems, Social Security was remarkably limited and conservative. Although the second New Deal provided increased federal regulation of banking, supervision of labor-management relations, and legislation to break up public utilities holding companies, at no point did it attempt to substitute central economic planning for the private decision-making of a free enterprise system. The New Deal sought to save capitalism by once again restraining excesses and by insisting that the individual worker be accorded pension, unemployment, and bargaining rights. One historian termed the second New Deal the creation of a welfare state on a capitalistic foundation. The American business system was antagonized, as Shouse's account makes clear, but its essential features of private decision-making and profit were saved.

Whatever else it accomplished, the second New Deal paved the way for Roosevelt's landslide reelection in 1936. The new wave of legislation encouraged liberals. Conservative opponents were frustrated when even Roosevelt's Republican challenger, Kansas Governor Alfred M. Landon, endorsed many New Deal programs. The extent of the New Deal's popularity in 1936 can be read in the election returns. Roosevelt won more than 60 percent of the presidential vote while over three-fourths of those elected to the new Congress were Democrats.

The 1936 election victory, ironically, carried the seeds of the New Deal's destruction. Encouraged by the manifestations of overwhelming support, Roosevelt decided to take radical steps to reform the Supreme Court which had recently overturned the NRA and AAA and was threatening to declare other New Deal legislation unconstitutional. To reduce the influence of several conservative justices who had served on the Court for years, Roosevelt suddenly proposed adding a judge for each member of the federal judiciary who failed to retire at the age of 70. This plan, which could have immediately given FDR six appointments to the Supreme Court, was quickly labeled the "Court-packing" bill. Opposition to the proposal came both from FDR's usual foes and many past New Deal supporters. Giving the president such influence over the Court, they argued, would upset the constitutional system of checks and balances, place tremendous — even dictatorial — power in the hands of the executive, and threaten civil liberties. During the spring of 1937 as the Court-packing controversy raged, Justice Owen Roberts began voting in favor of New Deal programs; the administration, therefore, began winning cases 5 to 4 instead of losing them by the same margin. Then an old conservative justice, Willis Van Devanter, decided to retire. With the appointment of Democratic Senator Hugo Black to the vacant seat, the Court was firmly in the hands of friendly judges. Four more Roosevelt appointments followed within three years. The New Deal never again faced a judicial threat. But the Court fight disenchanted some Roosevelt admirers, welded in Congress a conservative coalition of Republicans and southern Democrats who, having thwarted the Court-packing bill, were prepared to oppose FDR again and effectively brought the legislative activity of the New Deal to a close. A limited Fair Labor Standards Act, setting maximum hours and minimum wages for workers, and an act providing federal funds for construction of low-cost public housing, both passed in 1938, were the only significant New Deal legislative achievements after the Court battle.

Roosevelt's innate conservatism, mentioned by both Farley and Tugwell in their accounts, displayed itself in 1937. Always troubled by unbalanced government budgets, Roosevelt cut federal spending when it appeared to him that the economy was improving. Recovery had been achieved largely by government spending programs so that the loss of WPA and other funds, together with the siphoning of $2 billion in the new Social Security taxes, threw the still shaky economy into a downspin. In the last four months of 1937, unemployment increased by two million. Industrial output and stock prices fell sharply. Once again Americans suffered through a severe depression winter, only now it was blamed on Roosevelt not Hoover. After much deliberation, FDR in April, 1938, requested, and Congress soon approved, a nearly $4 billion spending program. During the summer, the economy began to show signs of improvement.

Ten years after the 1929 stock market crash, the New Deal clearly had not totally cured the depression. Industrial production and national income had finally climbed above 1929 levels, but more than 17 percent of the work force still lacked jobs. The idea took hold that several million might be permanently unemployed. The New Deal saved many bankers, depositors, farmers, businessmen, and destitute persons from disaster. Public funds employed millions while labor legislation helped other workers improve their lot through collective bargaining. Rex Murray and Elmer Powers seem to feel that the New Deal aided workers and farmers, but neither suggests that it ended their difficulties. Within a few years, it would become obvious that the New Deal simply did not go far enough, that much greater federal spending — the sort generated by war — was required to restore prosperity.

It also was apparent by the end of the 1930s that the reform program of the New Deal had been rather narrowly focused on economic matters. The Roosevelt administration generally ignored social reforms not related to economic recovery. One example was the case of black America. The New Deal was not anti-black. In fact, in contrast to previous administrations, FDR and several of his principal advisors expressed sympathy for the problems of blacks. Blacks responded by abandoning their traditional loyalty to the Republican party (the party of Abraham Lincoln) and, from 1936 onward, voting Democratic in overwhelming numbers. While Roosevelt wished that blacks be treated just as any other poor people in receiving the benefits of New Deal programs, it often proved difficult, especially in the South, to overcome the prejudices of lower level officialdom. Consequently, blacks received fewer economic benefits of the New Deal than their needs and numbers warranted. While Roosevelt called attention to the special social problems of blacks, discrimination, segregation, terrorism, lynching, and disfranchisement, he was unwilling to jeopardize his legislative programs, the fate of which rested in the hands of a largely Southern congressional leadership, in a political battle for remedies. NAACP Executive Secretary Walter White's account (chapter seven), a 1940 statement to a congressional committee, suggests that the New Deal had done little to alter the black's second-class citizenship which carried the constant fear and occasional reality of racial violence by whites.

For blacks as well as other Americans, World War II, far more than the New Deal, proved to be the great reformer. The war ended the depression, creating full employment and prosperity. Moreover, it stimulated enormous social change, opening opportunities to blacks and women in particular. The war prompted important alterations in the Presidency and the federal government and extended other changes which had begun in the 1930s.

The threat of war had been growing in Europe and Asia since the early 1930s as Germany, Italy, and Japan sought to expand their territories and power. Facing a vocal minority of Americans who favored isolationism as well as a general public distaste for war, Roosevelt hesitated to take forceful diplomatic steps. Even discussing foreign affairs to inform Americans of threats to the national interest FDR regarded as politically risky. Nevertheless, without fully confiding in the American people, the president took various executive actions which brought the United States to the brink of active participation in World War II. Neutrality laws, adopted by Congress in the mid-thirties to prevent American involvement in foreign conflicts, were manipulated in 1937 to help China resist a Japanese attack. In September, 1940, Roosevelt, lacking clear constitutional authorization, arranged with British Prime Minister Winston Churchill to exchange 50 World War I American destroyers needed to defend Great Britain for several British naval bases in the Western Hemisphere that ostensibly would bolster American security. The executive agreement, completed without consulting Congress, openly identified the U.S. with the British battle against Nazi Germany. Soon Roosevelt was exploring ways of providing more assistance to Britain. He argued that to lend or lease surplus war material to enemies of the German-Italian-Japanese Axis was as sensible as loaning a neighbor a garden hose to put out a house fire.

Congress approved a Lend-Lease program in March 1941. U.S. Navy convoying of lend-lease supplies led, by early autumn, to an undeclared shooting war between American vessels and German submarines in the North Atlantic. Also, since 1939 FDR had applied economic pressure on Japan to stop its attacks on China and its threats to Southeast Asia. In 1941 embargoes on exporting aviation fuel and scrap iron to Japan were followed by a freeze on all Japanese funds in the U.S. Japan's surprise attack on Pearl Harbor, December 7, 1941, followed within days by Germany's declaration of war on the U.S., concluded a long, slow movement toward war. That America's interests were best served by becoming actively involved in the battle against the Axis should not obscure the fact that President Roosevelt, concerned about congressional isolationism and doubtful of public support, took independent, often disguised steps to lend American assistance to the Allied cause.

Once war came, Roosevelt used the political skills acquired in domestic affairs to muster support for the war effort and to mobilize economic military power. He also worked to unify a disparate, often discordant group of allies including Great Britain, China, and the Soviet Union in the battle against the Axis. Even more than during the 1930s, the president became the nation's leader and the focus of attention while the federal government assumed a larger role in American life.

World War II became as much an economic struggle as a military one, at least for the United States. Actual casualties were limited, compared to those of other major participants. Of the perhaps 40 million persons who were killed (seven million soldiers and 13 million civilians of the Soviet Union alone), only about 350,000 were American. The U.S., alone among the major participants, was spared invasion and heavy bombing. Yet America made a substantial contribution to the war. In the words of Franklin Roosevelt, the U.S. became "the arsenal of democracy". The nation's industrial and agricultural production supplied Britain, the Soviet Union, and other allies as well as

America's own war effort. During the war, American industry produced 86,000 tanks, 296,000 airplanes, 11,900 ships, 64,000 landing craft, 15 million guns, four million tons of artillery shells, and 40 billion bullets. At the Yalta conference near the war's end, Joseph Stalin offered a toast to American industry without which, the Soviet premier asserted, the Allies never would have won the war.

Mobilizing the American economy to meet the war crisis required an unprecedented degree of government regulation. In January, 1942, Roosevelt established the War Production Board (WPB) to "exercise general responsibility" over the economy. The WPB supervised the conversion of industry to war production, often in the face of business resistance. Contracts were based on cost of production with an assured profit. The WPB set production quotas and allocated scarce resources. Other agencies oversaw other facets of the economy. The War Manpower Commission determined the apportionment of workers between industry and the armed forces. The National War Labor Board supervised labor-management relations, obtained a no-strike, no-lockout pledge from unions and business which reduced to a minimum (though it did not eliminate) production time lost due to labor disputes, and limited wage increases to 15 percent to halt inflation and job switching. Government regulation brought many problems, of course, and critics found plenty of opportunities to second guess. Many of the difficulties to be faced were especially evident in the synthetic rubber crisis. Since the Japanese had seized 90 percent of the world's natural rubber, a virtually new industry had to be created in the midst of competing powerful interests, technological uncertainties, and extreme time pressures. The 1942 statements of FDR and radio commentator Fulton Lewis, Jr., concerning rubber (chapter nine) reflect the confusion, differences of opinion, and eventual bureaucratic response to one particularly important problem of wartime economic regulation.

The rapid transition from depression to a wartime economy of heavy military spending, high production, full employment, and rising wages posed further economic problems. The spiraling deficits of a government fighting an enormously costly war, coupled with consumer demands in excess of the supply of goods, threatened to produce runaway inflation. Both to finance the war and to reduce consumer spending, the system of annual income tax payment was abandoned for the now-familiar practice of withholding taxes from every paycheck. The Office of Price Administration (OPA) was created to keep the civilian economy under control. The OPA placed limits on prices of consumer goods and established a coupon system for rationing scarce commodities. Forced to manage myriad details, the OPA became a bureaucratic nightmare, but it generally succeeded in its anti-inflationary purpose.

The great wartime need for workers presented unusual opportunities for blacks and women. A growing militance by black leaders such as A. Philip Randolph of the railway porters union increased opportunities for blacks. Randolph's threatened March on Washington in July 1941 caused the administration to create a Fair Employment Practice Committee (FEPC) to end discrimination in war industries and preserve racial peace. The manpower shortage itself did far more than FEPC to lead reluctant employers to hire blacks. The proportion of black workers in war industries rose from three percent in mid-1942 to eight percent three years later. Furthermore, the number of blacks in skilled jobs doubled, and semiskilled positions for blacks increased even more. The movement of black war workers into largely white communities produced racial tensions, most notably the 1943 Detroit race riot in which 25 blacks and nine whites were killed. The armed forces, rigidly segregated before the war, could not afford to waste manpower and gradually expanded opportunities for the more than one million blacks who entered the military. The navy did the most to integrate and to upgrade assignments for blacks. Still, not until the Korean War would the armed forces fully desegregate. World War II scarcely resolved the problems of black Americans, but the war did expand opportunities and awareness, creating a base for postwar advancement. As Walter White suggested in 1940, the U.S. found it awkward to oppose nazism and later communism without making some effort to end racism in America.

Women, like blacks, partially escaped their restricted status, and in many cases were not satisfied with a return to it after the war. Millions of women had worked before the war. But as with blacks, women, "the last hired and first fired," suffered disproportionately during the depression. The wartime demand for labor caused the number of employed women to rise from 13 million in 1940 to 19 million by 1944 so that they constituted 36 percent of the civilian labor force. At first women began to replace men in light work, but by 1943 they held many heavy jobs. The non-dainty image of "Rosie the Riveter" acquired by the five million women working in war industries was based on fact. In aircraft plants, for instance, women did most of the actual assembly work while men did most of the supervising. The American planes which bombarded Germany and Japan were predominately built by women. As the accounts (chapter ten) of federal officials Mary Anderson, Mary Elizabeth Pidgeon, and Margaret Hickey illustrate, women workers encountered various types of discrimination and were often quickly dismissed once men began to return. Wartime employment opened new vistas for many women by giving them a sense of independence and self-satisfaction which they had not known before.

While many benefitted from the war, others did not. Factories and military bases sprang up, creating jobs, but the influx of workers and soldiers as well as the economic changes disrupted stable communities. Employment and migration raised incomes and opened minds, but tore families apart (divorce increased from 16 per 100 marriages in 1940 to 27 per 100 by 1944; delinquency among juveniles, unsupervised by working parents, grew tremendously). Blacks and women gained better treatment, but Americans of Japanese and, to a lesser extent, German or Italian ancestry faced persecution. The war affected every section of the country, but the impact on the South was perhaps most extreme. The accounts of seven Louisianans (chapter eight) reveal some influences of wartime on a previously provincial and economically retarded region.

World War II changed the United States domestically, but it also altered America's international position. Prior to 1941, the U.S. had avoided assuming a leading role in world affairs. Even in World War I, the previous peak of American foreign involvement, the U.S. refused to join any alliance (fighting instead as an "associated power") and, once the war was over, declined to participate in the League of Nations which had been proposed by its own president. Following the attack on Pearl Harbor, the U.S. quickly abandoned these past habits. The U.S. not only joined but in many respects led the anti-Axis alliance.

Roosevelt acted as a mediator between those mutually suspicious allies, Winston Churchill of Britain and Joseph Stalin of the Soviet Union. As Assistant Secretary of State Adolf Berle points out in his account of Roosevelt's diplomacy (chapter eleven), some of the compromises made to further the war effort were distasteful but hastened the end of the struggle. He offers as an example relations with the Vichy French leader Admiral Jean Darlan during the 1942 invasion of North Africa. Roosevelt became increasingly convinced that a peaceful postwar world was possible if the alliance held together. To this end he exerted American leadership. FDR encouraged the creation of a new world organization, the United Nations, to be dominated by the major wartime allies. The president also was willing, as Berle indicates, to concede a good deal to Stalin at the Yalta conference in February 1945, in hopes of cementing good relations. Roosevelt's policy failed, due in no small part to the death (six weeks after his return from Yalta) of the president who argued in his fourth inaugural address that "to have a friend you have to be a friend." The Cold War quickly began to develop after FDR was succeeded by a more rigidly anti-communist and less optimistic Harry Truman. Yet FDR's intention that the U.S. assume a leading responsibility in world affairs became an accepted principle for the postwar decades.

Roosevelt's death, coming less than a month before the surrender of Germany and only four months before Japan's capitulation, ended an era. Postwar America would struggle to cope with a prosperous economy and a non-shooting conflict with communism, problems of a different sort than depression and world war. Nevertheless, the United States entered the post-1945 era deeply marked by the 12 years of the Roosevelt Presidency. As the accounts which follow show so vividly, the experiences and attitudes of those who lived through the years 1933 to 1945 varied considerably. None would deny, however, that to live in FDR's America was to live in extraordinary times.

James A. Farley and Franklin Roosevelt [International News Photo]

CHAPTER ONE

FDR the Man

JAMES A. FARLEY

Introduction by DAVID E. KYVIG

No man did more to help Franklin D. Roosevelt win the Presidency in 1932 than James A. Farley. An Irish Catholic born May 30, 1888, in the small Hudson River town of Grassy Point, New York, Farley's involvement in politics began at an early age. He was elected Democratic town chairman when only 21, and two years later he won a race for clerk in his heavily Republican home town. In 1918 he became Democratic county chairman and an active supporter of Alfred E. Smith, who won his first term as Governor of New York later that year. During Smith's 10-year domination of the New York Democratic party, Farley rose to the position of secretary of the state Democratic committee. In 1928 Smith won the Democratic presidential nomination and asked Franklin D. Roosevelt to strengthen the party ticket in New York by running for governor. Farley was put in charge of Roosevelt's New York City campaign headquarters. When Roosevelt won a close race while Smith was losing heavily, Farley was in a position to leave the falling star and join the rising one.

Governor Roosevelt soon made Farley chairman of the state Democratic party. After helping engineer the governor's landslide reelection in 1930, Farley immediately began to boost FDR for the 1932 presidential nomination. Possessed of an easy charm and an incredible memory for names and faces, Farley traveled around the country, building a network of Roosevelt supporters. At the hard-fought 1932 Democratic convention, Farley effectively marshalled FDR's forces on the floor, helped muster the votes which gave his candidate a fourth ballot nomination, and received a prompt reward by being chosen Democratic National Chairman. After managing the fall campaign which produced a landslide Democratic victory, Farley was named Postmaster General by President-elect Roosevelt.

During the eight years in which he served both in Roosevelt's cabinet and as party chairman, tall, bald, ever-smiling, "Big Jim" Farley was FDR's best known and most important political aide. He tirelessly lined up votes in Congress, kept in touch with party leaders throughout the country (signing all his letters with his characteristic green ink), and organized Roosevelt's sweeping reelection victory in 1936. In that year Farley greatly enhanced his reputation for political shrewdness with the surprising and absolutely correct pre-election prediction that Roosevelt would carry every state but two, Maine and Vermont.

After 1936, Farley and Roosevelt began drifting apart. FDR failed to consult Farley before announcing his plan to reorganize the Supreme Court in 1937, and he ignored his party chairman's advice in attempting to purge conservative Democrats in the 1938 congressional elections. Both initiatives proved politically disastrous. Farley in the meantime was developing his own presidential ambitions. He expressed opposition to the principle of a third term, about which Roosevelt was playing coy, saying that it would weaken the party by stifling the ambitions of younger men. Farley actively sought the Democratic nomination in 1940, and when FDR finally indicated his willingness to accept a draft, the chairman nevertheless allowed his own name to be put forth. After delegates cast 72 votes for Farley, 61 for Vice President John Nance Garner, and 946 for Roosevelt, Farley, ever the party loyalist, moved that FDR's nomination be made unanimous.

The third term battle brought an end to the long relationship between Farley and Roosevelt. Shortly after the convention, "Big Jim" resigned the national chairmanship as well as his cabinet position. He became chairman of the board of Coca-Cola Export Corporation, a post he held well into his 80s. His political activities were largely confined to appearances at party conventions and interviews in the press. Gradually, his disappointment faded.

James A. Farley — still vigorous, alert, and gracious at the age of 77 — talked about the personality of Franklin Roosevelt to undergraduates at Kalamazoo College in Michigan on August 5, 1965. Farley's rambling recollections provide a view of FDR by someone who observed him at close hand over many years and suggest some interesting questions. Was Farley, because of their association, able to judge Roosevelt objectively? Was Roosevelt merely an engaging personality skilled at political maneuver or was he committed to particular principles? Was his leadership cautious and compromising or forceful and decisive? Was his administrative approach of delegating the same task to two departments a means of achieving better results through competition or a sign of inefficiency and sloppiness? Was Roosevelt, as Farley claims, "deeply conservative?"

I shall endeavor to briefly tell you my relationship with Mr. Roosevelt and my association with him during those very troublesome years. As a matter of fact, you could talk all night about the man.

I knew him fairly intimately before he was stricken with polio. I remember full well every time I go into the Biltmore Hotel in New York City. I always picture the scene of my waiting at the top of those steps, maybe a dozen or more in number, for him to come up and me to greet him. Then he was to go up to my home town where he was going to deliver a Flag Day address on June 14. The following year [1921] he was stricken with polio, but I never go into the Biltmore Hotel in New York City and look at those steps, but I think of the days when he came up those steps two steps at a time. During all those years I was associated with him when he was stricken, I never heard him complain once about his ailment. A matter of fact, the only time I ever heard him refer to it was one night. We were playing cards in the White House, and there was a fellow playing with us named Steve Gibbons from New York who was an Assistant Secretary of the Treasury. We were playing a very mild poker game and, as we were proceeding to leave at the conclusion of the game that evening, the president looked at Steve and he said, "Steve, there is one thing that they can say about us, we'll never get high blood pressure from running upstairs." That's the only time I ever heard him make reference to his infirmity.

"FDR The Man," is a difficult assignment, because it is not easy to separate a man from his accomplishments. The personality of President Roosevelt is reflected in his first two administrations, rather than in his last two. In the last two, the compulsions of war and failing health assailed him. In his first two administrations, he had much more freedom of action.

A man may be judged in considerable part by whom he admires. President Franklin Delano Roosevelt had a tremendous admiration for his namesake predecessor, President Theodore Roosevelt. [Theodore Roosevelt was Franklin's fifth cousin as well as the uncle of FDR's wife, Eleanor. Although they were separated by 24 years in age, came from distant branches of the same family, and belonged to opposing political parties, the two men were acquainted. In fact, while president, Theodore gave away the bride at Eleanor and Franklin's wedding in 1905.] I do not presume to say that he patterned himself after the late President Theodore Roosevelt, because he had a unique personality of his own. But in many ways they were alike. Both had tremendous physical vitality. Both had suffered physical ailments, the overcoming of which required the full use of their native physical endowment. Both succeeded, itself an indication of willpower and of character. But I think that the zest for life transcended even this. There was a love of life, its problems and its contests, which made our many years together a daily joy. Parenthetically, it was only at the end of our long association that the feeling of playing on a great team together departed. And such severance took place on a basis of principle, not of personality, over the questions of a third term.

We were both upstaters, born Democrats in Republican strongholds. He was from Hyde Park in Dutchess County on the west bank of the Hudson. I was from a little community called Grassy Point in Rockland County, about 40 miles down the river on the opposite side and about 30 miles below the military academy at West Point. His animation and independence showed early. He fought the Republican machine and won in Dutchess. [FDR, then a young attorney, was asked by Dutchess County Democratic leaders to run for the state senate in 1910 against a Republican incumbent in a district which had only once since the Civil War elected a Democrat. A strenuous campaign and a split between conservative and progressive Republicans brought Roosevelt a narrow victory in his first political race.] He fought the Democratic state organization, then controlled by Tammany Hall, and prevented the election of their choice, William F. Sheehan of Buffalo, known as

"Blue-eyed Billy" Sheehan, for the United States Senate. In those days United States Senators from New York were elected by the state legislature. [In 1911, during his first weeks in the state senate, Roosevelt became the leader of a group of insurgent Democrats who opposed the Tammany candidate for senator. The revolt deadlocked the Democratic majority, drew national publicity, and eventually resulted in Sheehan's withdrawal. The victory was far from total, however, as the compromise candidate was another Tammany figure.]

He had a tremendous advantage at all times. Politics was the means of the expression of his views and his personality. It was never a means of his livelihood. Endowed, as was President Theodore Roosevelt, with the necessities of life, he approached public service as the duty of a man of preferred position. I call this, manifestations of this, unshakable confidence. It has been called the consciousness of effortless superiority and even arrogance by his detractors. I do not hold with them. I believe he was gifted with a sense of destiny and of leadership which stood him and the nation in good stead in the hour of a grave crisis.

Part of this confidence and part of this physical health resulted in the continuing atmosphere of almost boisterous good humor. As we planned the 1932 campaign, our relationship reminded me much of my baseball days at Grassy Point where I was born and raised. We were both in the best of health, and I say this despite the governor's polio handicap. And all was in good spirits. We both loved the game as teammates. If I may say so, we had a very fine personal relationship. So much has been written of our split that it has been overlooked that men must be very close, indeed, to have a split become first page news. I think I knew Mr. Roosevelt as well as any man and better than most, because, in the formative period particularly, Louis Howe, his former secretary and close friend, and I were the only ones, other than Mrs. Roosevelt, to whom he could possibly have opened his heart.

I always felt very sorry that Louis Howe was never given his just due for the services he performed for Mr. Roosevelt in the years when he was stricken with polio. He was his secretary, he was his nurse, so to speak, he was his close confidant, he handled all his mail, he handled everything that had to do with Mr. Roosevelt's affairs, and it was he, and he alone in my judgment, that kept Mr. Roosevelt's spirits high after being stricken as he was at his age with that dreadful disease. I always said if it hadn't been for Louis and the unselfish work that he did that Mr. Roosevelt never would have run for governor and been elected twice and would never have become President of the United States.

In his heart Mr. Roosevelt was a deeply good man. Superficially gay, he was really quite religious. He paid much attention to his trusteeship of St. James Church in Hyde Park even when under the heavy burden of the war.

His mind was extraordinarily quick. He instantly grasped the full implication of a political situation, moving instinctively much in the manner of a professional baseball player who shifts when the different batters come to the plate. Now, of course, depending on what side you are on, the adjectives vary. If you are for a fellow, you call him nimble and adroit. Your opponent, however, calls him unstable and mercurial. Mr. Roosevelt has been called both, but the point I am making is that both are describing the same qualities, and no matter how you add them up they come out with the same answer, that he was exceptionally canny, knowledgeable and had political savvy in the highest degree.

Now what were his objectives? I have always felt, first to live in history as a great president. He wanted to equal or surpass President Theodore Roosevelt and his old chief, President Woodrow Wilson, as a progressive. In this particular, I think, he took heed of President Wilson's political defeat on the League of Nations. He was much more compromising than Mr. Wilson. Mr. Wilson never really interested himself in the lower echelons of politics and really knew nothing about them. President Roosevelt did, and understood them better, much better, in fact as well as any man I have ever known. Now, it is amazing how little things cause bitterness and hatred to arrive with men in politics. One of the strongest Democrats in the Senate in Mr. Wilson's administration was a man named Senator James Reed of Missouri, one of the great political orators of his day. He and Mr. Wilson broke on the appointment of a postmaster in a large city in Missouri, because President Wilson would not give to Senator Reed what is regarded as the senator's privilege: the appointment of a postmaster in his city. They broke, and he became one of President Wilson's most severe critics and probably had as much to do as anyone else in bringing about the defeat in the Senate that caused our country to lose at Versailles.

Now this did not prevent Mr. Roosevelt from committing his more disastrous political blunder — the attack on the Supreme Court. But it did enable him to govern New York State during the Seabury investigation of the late Mayor James A. Walker's administration without assisting Judge Seabury in the least and without favoring the Democratic organization at all. [In 1931 and 1932, Governor Roosevelt faced a difficult situation as charges of corruption were leveled at the administration of New York City Democratic Mayor James J. Walker. To defend Walker would prompt Republicans and others to charge cover-up, to abandon him would alienate Tammany Hall, either course would damage FDR's chances for the Presidency. Roosevelt walked a tightrope, appointing Judge Samuel Seabury to conduct an investigation, avoiding comment as long as possible, and finally, in the course of hearings during the summer of 1932, pressuring Walker into resigning. The Republicans lost an issue, yet Tammany continued to support FDR.] Both sides assailed him, both called him the man on the flying trapeze, but neither sensed that he enjoyed that role very much. His sense that his place in history depended on what he did for the common man was called demagoguery by his opponents. I just won't accept this at all. I sat in at the early cabinet meetings. I can tell you there was no time for demagoguery. The hour was late, and the days were too full of anxiety for any thought other than the welfare of our country.

I am sure that those of you here and many people throughout this country often wonder what happens at cabinet meetings. Mr. Roosevelt held them regularly, at least once a week. One week it would be in the morning, so the afternoon papers would have the story of the cabinet meeting. The next week it would be in the afternoon, so the morning papers would have their opportunity to cover it. I never made any notes or tried to keep a record of what happened at those meetings, except several do stand out in my memory. Mr. Roosevelt would come in and greet everybody at the table, addressing each one by their first names as a rule, and then he would turn to Mr. [Cordell] Hull, the Secretary of State, and ask him if he had anything he wanted to say to the cabinet. Most of the time he didn't. As a matter of fact, very few of the cabinet members talked very much except Mr. [Secretary of Commerce Daniel C.] Roper and Miss [Secretary of Labor Frances] Perkins, and both of them when they spoke had something to say. I will never forget one day at a cabinet meeting. Mr. [Vice President John Nance] Garner, who was prone at times to become a little garrulous, but in my judgment one of the greatest men I have ever known, much misunderstood by the people generally, one day started to talk about the income tax which most people now are not in favor of and most people apparently were not much in favor of then. But Mr. Garner started telling about the passage of the act back in '24 or thereabouts [actually, 1913]. At the time of the passage of the bill, apparently he was very much opposed to it and did all he could to prevent the bill from becoming enacted into law. But this day he was praising Cordell Hull for what he had done in connection with that legislation. Mr. Hull apparently wasn't listening — he was reading some papers on his lap — without looking up said, "John, it took you a long time to reach that opinion," knowing full well that Garner had opposed it.

Now in those days the banks had been closed and re-opened, but they were very shaky. Millions were jobless, and millions were hungry. Those pieces of legislation pounded out in the face of imminent national danger were entrusted in a large measure to me operating as chairman of the Democratic National Committee to effectuate the passage of those bills on the Hill. Many men took part in their formation, and it is significant, as the late Speaker Sam Rayburn has pointed out many times, that of the hundred-odd basic acts, such as labor legislation, banking reforms, securities regulation, social security and many others, not one was ever repealed, and all have been augmented by both parties in succeeding sessions of the Congress. Accordingly it is unkind, unfair, and untrue to call Mr. Roosevelt a demagogue on this or any other score. To be sure, he loved the approval of the people and the lionization by his following — but frankly who doesn't? Loving applause and rabble-rousing are two different things.

There are two factors which prevented FDR from becoming a rabble-rouser. First, and you may believe me, he was deeply conservative. He hated to spend public money unnecessarily, and he dreamed of the day he could balance the budget. I shall always remember an evening I spent with him after dinner in the White House, as he was going over with me matters which of necessity required his approval. I shall never forget when he said if the price of cotton, which I think then was about six cents a pound in the market, could be raised to 10 or 11 cents and corn and wheat could be raised from the price offered in the Kansas City markets, comparable with the increase in cotton, and if it were possible to increase the national income from approximately, as I recall it, 57 to 60 billion dollars at that time to approximately 75 billion dollars, we would have been able to balance the budget, and if my memory serves me correctly, the budget that year was something between 7 and 8 billion dollars. Now we have a budget of over 80 billion dollars, upwards of 40 of which has to do with the Department of Defense, about 5½ billions are for interest on the war debt, and, in the year I referred to, the budget was about a little better than seven billion dollars. The public needs and the necessity of spending held his mind, but close to his heart was the idea of stopping federal spending as quickly as he could. At the slightest rise in the economic health of the country, he would stop spending. In fact he stopped spending so abruptly in 1937 that it brought about a recession.

Perhaps nothing illustrates how conservative he was at heart than the discovery that the ex-president of the New York Stock Exchange, Richard Whitney, was an embezzler. Had Mr. Roosevelt been a demagogue he would have gone to the country screaming, "I told you so," and demanded fuller powers. He could have gotten them, too. But he did nothing of the kind. Perhaps it is an index to FDR the man that tears came to his eyes. "I can't believe, that Dick Whitney would do such a thing," he said and added, "poor Groton." Mr. Roosevelt and Mr. Whitney were classmates at Groton before they both went to Harvard.

One of his great qualities was to turn reverses into a joke. Thus when he lost the purge elections in 1938, defeating only one opponent, the Chairman of the Rules Committee, John O'Connor of New York, he laughed off his defeat with the marvelous wisecrack "It was a bad season, but we won the Yale game." Another time his executive secretary, the very able James Rowe, urged him to take action to which he was opposed. According to Jim Rowe, the president said, "Jim, you made a very forceful argument, but by accident we are not going to do it." "By accident?" asked Rowe, "what accident?" "The accident that the people of the United States elected me president, instead of you."

I told you that he was a man who could throw off a jibe. But there was one that cut him deeply. That came at a time that he was convinced that the country had to prepare for war. Taking the cue from his agricultural plan of reducing crops by a third, the president's foreign policy was described on the Senate floor as a plan "to plow under every third American boy." Now that hurt and hurt him deeply, so deeply that it was weeks before he rallied to become very angry about it.

He liked nothing better than new ideas and interesting people, and he especially liked to talk to them over the cocktail at the day's end, and frankly, he fancied himself, and I say this as a non-drinker, that he was a great cocktail mixer, with few equals in martinis and without parallel in old-fashioneds.

He was deeply aware of the perogatives of the Presidency. He insisted that the great respect for the office be observed, because none respected it more than he. Thus he was annoyed when an autograph seeker somehow or other presumed to go upstairs in the White House to get his autograph. He refused and ordered the young man expelled from the White House.

Although his life had been attempted in Miami, it affected him little. [On February 15, 1933, while FDR was vacationing in Florida, an unemployed bricklayer named Joseph Zangara began shooting at the president-elect who was sitting in an open car. Roosevelt was unscathed, but several persons standing nearby were hit, and Chicago Mayor Anton J. Cermak eventually died from his wounds. Zangara was judged sane and subsequently executed for the murder of Mayor Cermak.] He was fatalist about that, and, as I have previously said, he was deeply religious. He often said, "If they want you, they will get you, and there isn't anything you can do about it." In fact, it was the cabinet which intervened to put more protection around him. The Attorney General, Robert H. Jackson, was summoned to the White House one midnight and found only one guard between Pennsylvania Avenue, and the Lincoln Room. He protested strongly and after that Mr. Roosevelt consented to more security measures.

He, of course, loved the navy because of his boyhood

sailing days. He also, of course, had been Assistant Secretary of the Navy under President Wilson, a job also held at one time by President Theodore Roosevelt. With his admirals he was in especially close contact. He could take criticism of his other departments very well, but those attacking the navy were walking on thin ice. He would shut off those critics with a single sentence: "What do they know about battleships?"

His administration has been described as the greatest royal court since Louis XIV. There is a certain element of truth about this. While the president was bold in imagination, swift in execution, and highly knowledgeable about government finance, administration was not one of his strong points. He was little less than grand in his delegation of authority and he was magnificent in backing up the men he appointed, but unfortunately he often appointed two departments with sweeping powers to do the same job.

His methods of reaching policy decisions in those early days is worthy of note. I have for it the greatest admiration. He would invite all points of view to the White House for dinner. Immediately thereafter, he would introduce the subject for discussion and then listen to all sides. Sometimes after 11 o'clock he would turn to Miss [Marguerite "Missy"] LeHand, his secretary, and say "Missy, I think this is the best we can do." He would then and there dictate his ideas in a memorandum. All had had their say, and all had the precise idea of what the president wanted. Thereafter, very frequently, he would delegate the job to two competing departments, and, from that moment on, the fur would start to fly. But his idea of administration stopped there.

His kitchen cabinet often had more access than the regular cabinet. [Harry L.] Hopkins and [Thomas G.] Corcoran were his principal lieutenants after the death of Louis Howe [in 1936] and, to the annoyance of many department heads, their word was law more often than not, and it caused considerable difficulties. It is a pattern that these two wise men ended up at loggerheads as did many of his departmental heads. This dislike of ordinary channels led him to value new faces and new ideas. In that respect he was very typical of the age in which he was educated. He had a little knowledge of nearly everything. He was an avid reader with a great memory. There was scarcely a subject onto which he could not contribute an anecdote or an observation. This accounts in part for his great personal charm. The experts of the country who had spent lifetimes on a particular subject would find that FDR knew enough about it to grasp immediately what they were talking about. This wide range of interest, these smatterings, if you will, gave Mr. Roosevelt the ability to be a great and a sympathetic listener without which quality he could not have been the justly famous conversationalist that he was.

If he had a single great love, I believe it was American history. On this he was an authority as is President Truman. For Mr. Roosevelt it had the excitement of a contest. One could almost see him visualizing himself how he would have acted had he been president at that time. He had a generally deep affection for our country, regarding it as the greatest romance of history. That spirit, I think, characterized his administration while I was in his cabinet. One almost felt the warm and keen interest in the administrations since George Washington. And here I will say that in my opinion there has never been an administration — Republican or Democrat — with that kind of attitude. The cabinet and the President of the United States are in our history majestic, and I never knew a man holding such position who did not give the country the best that was in him. I have no patience with those cynics who believe that there is no such a thing as consecrated public service. I have said that it is difficult to separate the man from the work, and it is. By their work shall you know them. And if this be the standard, FDR stands anchored in American history with the rest of our great presidents. As for FDR the man and myself, I have this to say. Since it is fair to say that we parted on a principle, it also follows that we met on a principle, the principle of what was best for New York State and later the nation. For 12 full years we saw the result of our labors enacted into laws which still stand as the laws of our country, laws which are now endorsed in the platforms of both political parties. Further the pattern of concern for our fellow Americans has been elaborated to a principled and permanent goal of this nation. None of these would have been possible without President Franklin D. Roosevelt, and so it is my conviction that Franklin Delano Roosevelt, the man, can safely rest his case before God, the American people, and history on the works and deeds of Franklin D. Roosevelt, the 32nd President of the United States.

CHAPTER TWO

FDR
and the Depression

REXFORD G. TUGWELL

Introduction by DAVID E. KYVIG

Rexford Guy Tugwell was perhaps the most radical and certainly one of the most controversial of Franklin Roosevelt's close associates. As a member of FDR's original campaign "Brain Trust" in 1932 and later as a presidential advisor on a wide range of matters, Tugwell had considerable influence during the first years of the New Deal. Although Tugwell left the administration at the end of 1936, he maintained contact with Roosevelt until the president's death in 1945.

Rex Tugwell was born July 10, 1891, in northwestern New York, the son of a cattle dealer, orchard farmer, and fruit and vegetable canner. At 18, he entered the University of Pennsylvania where he gradually focused his attention on agricultural economics. He earned his Ph.D. in 1922. He became an instructor at Columbia University in 1920, published widely over the next dozen years, and rose rapidly to become a full professor by 1931. Critical of the self-seeking individualism of American business and of governmental support for laissez faire capitalism, Tugwell increasingly advocated "social management" of the economy, centralized, rational allocation of resources to cause business and industry to better serve the public interest. Tugwell attributed the economic collapse of the early 1930s primarily to the expansion of production and rise of prices in previous years without an equivalent distribution of profits to workers. These factors caused a relative decline of purchasing power. Opposed to nationalizing industry, he nonetheless regarded "planned capitalism" as necessary for the restoration of economic health.

Early in 1932, Tugwell was recruited by another Columbia professor, Raymond Moley, to advise presidential candidate Franklin Roosevelt on farm economics. With Moley and Adolf A. Berle, Tugwell met repeatedly with FDR. The group, quickly dubbed the "Brain Trust" by a journalist, later wrote campaign speeches and offered economic strategy to the Democratic candidate. After Roosevelt's election, Tugwell urged the appointment of Henry A. Wallace of Iowa, publisher of *Wallaces' Farmer*, as Secretary of Agriculture and was himself asked to become assistant secretary.

During the first months of the New Deal, Tugwell contributed significantly to the formation of economic policy. He played an important role in drafting the Agricultural Adjustment Act and the National Industrial Recovery Act, the famous NRA, both of which implemented a degree of central economic planning. Gradually, however, other presidential advisors who did not seek changes in the institutional arrangements of capitalism but sought to restore confidence in the business system came to prevail. They proposed to check business abuses with banking and securities legislation and to protect individuals in a business economy with such devices as Social Security and the National Labor Relations Act of 1935. Tugwell, who thought more fundamental change was necessary, called this approach "planting protective shrubbery on the slopes of a volcano."

Critics of the New Deal and opponents of central economic planning increasingly made Tugwell their target, calling his theories of planned capitalism socialistic or communistic. The drug industry attacked him severely for proposing new food and drug legislation which included increased federal regulation of misleading advertising. When Roosevelt nominated Tugwell to the newly-created post of Undersecretary of Agriculture in 1934, several senators used the confirmation proceedings to label him a radical and a subversive. Although Tugwell won confirmation, he was becoming a liability for an administration sensitive to charges that its political philosophy was "far left." In 1935, FDR named Tugwell to head the Resettlement Administration, an agency to consolidate rural relief activities. Although the RA was primarily engaged in rehabilitation loans and education for poor farmers, Tugwell exhibited great interest in experimental programs to purchase and remove from use 9,000,000 acres of submarginal land, find better economic opportunities for displaced farmers in small cooperative communities, and establish planned, suburban "greenbelt" towns. Opponents charged that these RA

programs smacked of collectivization. Feeling that his influence with Roosevelt had waned and unhappy that his
radical reputation had prompted the Democrats to keep him
offstage during the 1936 campaign, Tugwell resigned from the
government at the end of that year.

Tugwell remained active following his departure from
Washington. He chaired the New York City Planning Commission from 1938 to 1940. Roosevelt appointed him Governor of Puerto Rico in 1941, a position which he filled with
distinction until 1946. For 11 years thereafter, Tugwell held a
professorship of political science at the University of Chicago.
Subsequently, he has been a fellow at the Center for the
Study of Democratic Institutions at Santa Barbara, California.

In a lecture at Kalamazoo College on July 15, 1965,
Tugwell commented on the depression and the first four years
of the Roosevelt Presidency. His observations on several
important issues raise thought-provoking questions. What
were the causes of the depression, as Tugwell saw them? Are
other explanations, for instance those of the Hoover administration, more satisfactory? Did the New Deal substantially
reform or help preserve the American business system? Was
Franklin Roosevelt's greatest accomplishment, as Tugwell
asserts, giving the American people hope?

To speak about the domestic problems of the age of Roosevelt
is such a large subject that I am sort of at a loss as to how to
begin. Perhaps there are a few of you who remember those
days, but not very many. There can't be very many. It is a
generation and a half or so ago and most young people don't
know what a depression is. I suppose — I hope — that you never
will know. It was something terrible. It was an experience which
the country had never undergone before quite to that extent,
although there have been hard times. It was one which nobody
seemed to know what to do about.

In 1932 when President Roosevelt was about to be
nominated for the Presidency by the Democratic party, he
began to study intensively what the depression was all about. It
was at that time that he began to make up his mind what his
policies would be if he should become president. And he was
pretty optimistic about it. He expected to become president. I
thought that perhaps the best thing I could do would be to say

what the view of things was at that stage, to say then what they were somewhat later when the New Deal began and he was actually president, and then to perhaps to follow through and to see what had happened to these policies later on. Not all of them persisted and some of them were not approved generally, especially by the Supreme Court. For the sake of simplification or putting things in categories, perhaps I could speak of them in three categories. Perhaps I could speak of relief and recovery and of reform. Practically all of the policies of those years fall under those categories. There are a few of them which fall outside, and I don't know how to categorize those in one word. Perhaps they fall under reform to a certain extent. Perhaps you would call them reorganization or something of the sort. I'll mention them a little later.

This first stage, when President Roosevelt began to make up his mind what his policy ought to be, came at a time when the country was at this low stage of economic activity. Well, there practically wasn't any economic activity. Things were very, very difficult indeed. The country seemed to have fallen into a paralysis from which it couldn't struggle out, and nobody knew what to do. Of course, there were a good many people who had advice to give, but they didn't seem very confident about their advice, and nobody was very confident about taking it. Nothing much was being done.

There were, of course, political reasons for this. You understand that President Hoover when he had been inaugurated in 1928 was supposed to be a very great man indeed, a great economist, and he was very generally called a great engineer. He had had a most remarkable career as a public philanthropist, if I may call him that. He had been the man who organized the relief work which was done for Belgium during the war when it was under German occupation. Then after the war he had organized it for most all of Europe and a great deal of Russia. It had been a tremendous and immense job. Then he had been made food administrator under President Wilson, and he had done a most remarkable job there. Then, of course, when the Republicans came in after Wilson, he had been nominated by President Harding to be Secretary of Commerce, and he had been Secretary of Commerce for eight Republican years before he ran for the Presidency and was elected in 1928.

Well, the years between the war and 1929 were years when

the great efficiencies which were discovered when the United States went to war were making their mark on the American economy. This was the time when the scientific management movement first made itself felt in the American economy. Efficiency was something which had never been known before. The output of goods was overwhelming so that there were surpluses of goods in almost every line by 1928. There was a great pile of debts. Everybody seemed to owe everybody else. When prices began to fall on account of the surpluses that couldn't be distributed, then it seemed like nobody was going to be able to pay his debts. And if he couldn't pay his debts, this meant that all the institutions with which he was connected were either bankrupt or potentially bankrupt. This was true not only of the banks who had loaned funds and couldn't get the funds back, so couldn't pay their depositors, but it was also true of insurance companies. All the fiduciary relationships were jeopardized in this way. It was a very difficult time.

It was just the kind of thing that you simply can't imagine happening in the United States, where we are supposed to be so inventive and so vigorous and to be so individually energetic. Yet during this time nobody could think of what to do. Bankers sat in their banks and folded their hands while everything crumbled around them. Factories closed down, discharged their employees, and stopped making goods. I used to travel in those days, on the governor's business at that time, a great deal from New York to Washington. I would go to the whole distance with only two or three people in the whole train with me. Looking out the window you would see factory after factory with its doors locked and no steam or smoke coming out of its chimneys. It was a tragic time.

There were, according to Frances Perkins, nearly 15 million men unemployed. Well, now if you multiply 15 by 4½ or five, you get the idea of how many people there were who had no income. In those days, you must remember there was no social security, no unemployment insurance. There were none of these things. If there wasn't any private charity, there wasn't anything, and of course private charity by 1932 had long since been exhausted. Not only private charity had been exhausted, but the funds of the states had been exhausted too. In New York Governor Roosevelt had the year before in 1931 set up a temporary emergency relief administration which took care of as many unemployed as it could. It soon ran out of funds because the relief load in New York State was so overwhelming and grew so fast that it was impossible to carry it out. During this time there was a great argument which went back and forth between President Hoover and members of Congress who were of various kinds of opinions about what ought to be done. But the people who bothered him most and needled him most were the progressives who felt that the federal government ought to make grants to the states so that the states could go on giving relief at least and perhaps set up programs of public works.

President Hoover, when he had been Secretary of Commerce, had studied this whole situation, studied the business cycle, and had a famous committee report to him about the business cycle. Nobody understood it better than he did. He had also set up a public works administrator to work up a shelf of public works to be used in just such circumstances as these. And they were used, but they were like a drop of water in the sea. They were overwhelmed by the problem. Nothing was large enough — could be large enough — to stem the paralysis that was overcoming the country.

When Senator Robert LaFollette and a few others who were the progressives in the Senate formulated bills to establish relief administrations and to make grants to the states with federal funds, President Hoover balked. He said, "We won't make grants to them, we will only make loans to them." This was because he had a theory that the federal government ought not to be responsible for the relief of any individual. He was a great believer in individualism. He had written a book called *Individual Initiative* [actually *American Individualism* (1922)] and "rugged individualism" was a phrase which he had used a great deal. Of course, it is now being used in reverse against him.

The situation was such that the president and the Congress had reached a standoff. The president wouldn't sign any bill that Congress passed, and the Congress wouldn't give in to the president's way of doing things. In the election of 1930, President Hoover was in such difficulties that he lost control of the House of Representatives, and it went Democratic. The Senate would have been Democratic if there had been one more senator elected by the Democrats. As it was, there were enough Democrats and progressives [Republicans] together so that they did control the Senate. So President Hoover couldn't get anything done in Congress if he had wanted to. Of course, the Congress couldn't persuade the president to do anything.

The situation was very bad. The Wall Street crash, of course, occurred in 1929, and banks began to close their doors all over the country because they couldn't meet their obligations. By 1932 many of the financial institutions were known to be potentially bankrupt if they were ever called on to meet the obligations they might have to meet. So anybody that came to the White House in the year 1933 was sure to meet the worst economic crisis that the country had ever had. Well, what to do in these circumstances? This was the problem that President Roosevelt was sure to face.

But first, of course, he faced the problem of what to do in the campaign. What should he say in the campaign about what he intended to do? Well, now there were several schools of thought about this. Almost everybody agreed that something had to be done about relief. This quarrel which had gone on so long about whether the federal government should enter the picture and provide funds for relief was practically resolved. Everybody knew now that the states had run out of funds, that private charity couldn't do anymore, and that the federal government would have to come in. So there wasn't any doubt about promising during the campaign that the federal government would establish a relief organization of some sort and would make grants to the states and provide public works. This wasn't really an issue anymore except that the Republicans were stubborn and stuck to it, and this gave the president a very good talking point, of course.

About other things on the issue of recovery, this was quite a different matter. There were several different theories from which he might choose one or from which he might choose parts of one. One of these theories was quite an old one which American economists had inherited from certain British economists like John S. Hobson and others. This was sometimes called the over-savings theory. In general what it meant was that there wasn't enough purchasing power allowed to consumers by producers in order to buy the goods the producers had made. Let me say that in a different way. When goods are produced, presumably the goods that are produced produce the income with which the goods can be bought. The people who make them get wages and the people who buy them, pay for them. So that, presumably, this is a complete circle. If that circle is broken somewhere and the producers take too much out in profits and don't pay enough wages, then the wage earners can't buy the share that they ought to be buying. Production has to close down or slow down because not enough consumers exist for the product. This was one theory, and it was a theory which was widely held by economists in this country. You see how well this went along with the theory that there ought to be relief for the unemployed just on humanitarian grounds because there was so much suffering and so many people were in misery. So the president had no hesitation in adopting this as one of his theories of recovery.

This, however, curiously enough, didn't suit the businessmen at all. The businessmen, bankers, and their economists didn't agree with this. Their theory was that the whole trouble was a lack of confidence. They said that the trouble was the businessmen were frightened of what the government was doing and what it might do, and that it was necessary for businessmen to be reassured so that they would begin to take chances again. If they took risks and they built new factories and they made more goods, then there would be more employment and people who were employed would get wages and they would buy the goods. This was a theory which didn't stand up very well because you could say that there had been eight years of businessmen's government, that is to say, Republican government. If businessmen were to have confidence in anybody, surely it would be President Hoover. This was a theory which was very widely held among businessmen and was used by President Hoover during the campaign. Of course, what he said was that the reason recovery didn't come was because everybody was afraid the Democrats were going to win. This suited the businessmen — or the businessmen who supported the Republicans — well enough, but it didn't convince very many people, as the election showed.

So much for theories of recovery. It was quite clear, I think, from the campaign that if President Roosevelt was elected there would be use of the federal government for relief purposes. In fact he said so a number of times during the campaign. He said he believed that the government existed in order to support its citizens when they were in need. If he were made president he would bring the forces of the government to the relief of people who had been in misery so long. President Hoover, on the other hand, said just the opposite. He said it was the people's business to support the government, and the government should never at any time support the people. This would be the ruination of individualism and initiative. That was the issue during the campaign.

Now so much for relief, so much for recovery. As to reform, there were different theories about this too. President Hoover had said a number of times during his administration that he thought that some reforms were needed in the financial world, in the bankers' world, in the stock market, and in the whole body of financial arrangements generally. One of the evils was that the bankers were taking their depositors' funds and speculating with them. They had their commercial banking and their long-term banking under the same hat and when they took funds in a fiduciary capacity, they simply loaned them for enterprises which they wanted to carry on themselves. They got to doing it for speculative purposes. A good many bankers, you know — well not a good many, but quite a few bankers — went to jail for this before this business was over. President Roosevelt made a good deal of it during the campaign and said that this was one of the reforms which would have to be made and that this was one of the sore spots in the economy. He attacked the business community pretty strongly on these grounds. This was something which the politicians were very leery about, and they often cautioned him. Before the campaign was over, he began to make a distinction between financiers and speculators and little businessmen. He said he didn't mean to attack little business-men; they were getting almost as bad a deal as the workers were in this. He sorted them out in that way, so that I think he got a great deal of support from the business community. In fact, there was a Businessmen's League for Roosevelt which got a great deal of support, and some very famous persons, after-wards, gave large amounts of money to this league. One of them was the father of President Kennedy, Joseph Kennedy, who was a member of the Businessmen's League for Roosevelt.

Then, of course, President Roosevelt was elected, and in 1933, when he took office, all of the banks in the country were closed. [Bank closings began on February 14, 1933, when Michigan Governor William Comstock declared a bank holiday to prevent a run on state banks as a result of rumors that major

Detroit banks were near collapse. Panic spread rapidly. Other states proclaimed holidays. By Roosevelt's inauguration on March 4, banks had closed in 38 states and were operating under restrictions on withdrawals elsewhere.] He declared a bank holiday until something could be done to reestablish the banking situation. Generally speaking, he appointed the people to sort out those institutions which could be said to be solvent and could go on from those who had used up their funds and couldn't hope to pay back their depositors. They simply stayed closed, and the others were allowed presently to reopen. [The Banking Act of 1933, providing for inspection of banks and reopening of those which were sound, was passed by both houses of Congress and signed by the president on March 9, the first day of a special session of Congress. By March 15, half of the nation's banks, holding 90 percent of all deposits, were open.]

The Reconstruction Finance Corporation was set up to make loans to banks who were potentially solvent but whose assets were frozen. [The Reconstruction Finance Corporation was established under the Hoover administration in January, 1932, to lend money to banks, railroads, and other businesses threatened with collapse. At first the RFC proceeded cautiously. The Roosevelt administration quickly enlarged the resources and activities of the RFC to help stimulate recovery.] This was one of the difficulties in those days, of course. There were plenty of banks and plenty of financial institutions which owned stocks, owned bonds, owned real estate, owned lots of things — but what was the use of owning them if you couldn't sell them? And you couldn't sell them if your depositors demanded their funds. You had the assets, but you didn't have the funds and you couldn't pay. So you were potentially solvent but not actually so. The Reconstruction Finance Corporation was set up to do this part of the job and did it. Gradually, over a period of a few months and perhaps a year, most of the banks which were solvent and had been behaving themselves were reopened and business went on.

About the reform part, however, the president didn't stop with just denouncing the speculators and the people who had mixed up their commercial banking with the long-run banking. He went on and formulated two or three laws which were very drastic in their reorganization of the banking system and the

Federal Reserve system. These laws were passed during the first year. One of the things that was done was to set up the Securities and Exchange Commission to oversee the stock market and to see that the gambling which had gone on there was put on a different basis. During the new era when speculation was going on so much, people could buy stocks on a very small margin. [This was the system by which an investor could put up a portion of the purchase price of a stock, "the margin," and borrow the balance with the stock as collateral. This could bring great profits if the price of the stock rose, but heavy debt if the price fell.] This was one of the things that had to be stopped and changed. You could buy stocks in those days on a 10 percent margin. Of course this allowed you to speculate and buy a large number of stocks with a small amount of funds. You could lose a lot too. Because speculation was so wild in those days, this contributed to the swaying and rocking of the whole economic system. This, of course, had to be stopped and was stopped by the various banking measures which were passed and by the Securities and Exchange Commission's regulations.

So much for reform of that sort. Now there are some other reforms which I don't know if you would call them reforms or not — they don't exactly fall into that category. They were very important in New Deal days. I don't know where you would put Social Security, for instance. I don't know whether you would call that a reform or a reorganization or exactly what you would call it. But Social Security was a very important part of President Roosevelt's policy, and he had intended it to be right along. He was well aware that social security systems had been established in Europe, in Germany for two generations, and of course, in England for at least a generation. He saw no reason why it shouldn't be extended to the United States. Of course, it proved to be very popular, although there were loud cries of communism and this sort of thing. It was the issue which was chosen to attack Roosevelt with in the campaign of 1936, four years later. This was the issue on which the campaign really was fought — that the New Deal was taking the country into a socialistic or communistic era and that all of this ought to be reversed. And of course, contrary to all precedents, the president won an overwhelming second victory in 1936.

Usually in these circumstances, in the second trial, the president loses pretty badly, and he loses sometimes in the congressional elections two years after he is elected, so that he loses control of Congress. You know how popular President Eisenhower was, but after his first two years as president he never had a Congress which had a majority of his own party. He had to work with Democrats for all of six years while he was in the White House. This didn't happen to Roosevelt, curiously enough. Something else happened to him which was just as bad. The Democratic party continued to win, but the Democratic party didn't approve of Roosevelt, that is to say, not all of it. There soon formed a coalition in Congress between the Republicans and southern conservatives which checkmated the president just as effectively as though there had been a Republican majority. After his overwhelming victory of 1936, he undertook reorganization of the Supreme Court and suffered one of the worst defeats of his entire career, by a coalition of Democrats from the south, the conservative Democrats — not all from the south, some from the north — and the Republicans. He was very badly defeated in this.

His efforts during his first term had one particular kind of policy which I would like to refer to specially. That is the setting up of the organization which was called the NRA, National Recovery Administration. This administration was an attempt to find a way in which business could be controlled by controlling itself, allowing businesses to bargain with each other up to a certain extent and from then on to have government control and planning of what their activities should be. This is a very short and inadequate explanation of what the NRA was. It was really a reversal of the old policy of automatic regulation through the anti-trust acts and free enterprise and free competition and that kind of thing. This was declared unconstitutional by the Supreme Court, you'll remember, and this was one of the reasons why the president thought in 1937 that the court ought to be reorganized. He said it was out of step with its time. It was a horse and buggy court. This didn't succeed, and the NRA was disestablished and was never reestablished, so that this policy was given up entirely. We are today right where we were then with respect to the regulation of business.

Agriculture which was another special thing which ought to be spoken of, had been in a bad way, not only during the depression years when everyone else was depressed, but from

1921 on. And it happened in this way. During the war, the American farmers were urged to increase their production, and they did. They increased it immensely. They succeeded in feeding all the armies plus most of Europe all during the war. Then, of course, after the war that market was gone. The soldiers came back to the land, and Europe began to raise its own food again. It not only didn't want American wheat and cotton, but wouldn't take it. They had agricultural policies of their own; they wanted to be self-sufficient. This made a very difficult situation for American farmers who had gotten themselves set up and had expanded their holdings in order to meet this great worldwide demand, then found it had disappeared. Immense surpluses began to build up.

There had been a farm block formed in the Congress to try to find some relief for American farmers. They had worked for years, and they had passed two or three bills which had been vetoed by President Coolidge and President Hoover. [The McNary-Haugen bills, vetoed by Calvin Coolidge in 1927 and 1928, represented the farm bloc's principal proposal for dealing with farm surpluses during the 1920s. A high tariff would be placed on agricultural imports, a government corporation would buy at the domestic price the unsold surplus after domestic needs had been met, and then the surplus would be sold on the world market. Costs would be paid from a fee on all producers, and thus, in theory, American farmers would be able to dispose of their entire crop at better than the world market price.] But President Hoover had finally given in in 1930 and set up what was called the Farm Board. [The Federal Farm Board, established June 15, 1929, loaned money to farmers' marketing cooperatives and established corporations to stabilize crop prices by large-scale buying and selling.] This Farm Board was supposed to take care of the surpluses by buying them and storing them or getting rid of them. But the Farm Board couldn't sell abroad anymore than the individual farmers or merchants could sell abroad, so it was a complete failure. The surpluses were still hanging over the market. Wheat went down to 25 cents a bushel, cotton to six cents a pound, and pork to a comparable level, so that farmers in the United States went on farming for nothing. They were burning wheat in their furnaces, or they were piling it up in the fields and it was rotting. Nobody knew what to do about the situation. It was a funny thing about farmers. They are very stubborn people, and, although everyone of them knew that production had to be decreased in order to meet the conditions of the existing American demand, one thing they demanded of any scheme which was outlined to them for agricultural relief was that it should not curtail production. This was politically very dangerous, and no politician ever dared say that he was going to cut down on production because farmers wouldn't like it. They were afraid farmers wouldn't vote for them if they did. This was the beginning of the voluntary domestic allotment scheme which President Roosevelt adopted and which was outlined vaguely somewhat during the campaign and which during the first months of his New Deal became the Agricultural Adjustment Administration. This administration set up farmers' committees all over the country and allowed them to vote as to whether they would reduce their acreage to the amount needed to meet the American market or not. It then set up county committees in order to administer the act. This succeeded in getting around the farmer's objection to cutting their production. Of course, there was another little gadget attached to it: the farmers were paid for not producing. This helped a great deal to settle their consciences about not using their land to the greatest extent possible.

I have dwelt almost altogether on the economic phases of the domestic policy of President Roosevelt because these were depression years and this was the problem. I don't know whether you can imagine — well, I'm sure you can't imagine if you haven't see it — what the spring of 1932 must have been like after three winters of depression and unemployment of this sort. You know we make a great to do if there are four million or five million unemployed. Can you imagine in a country with about half the population we have now what it must have been like to have 13-14-15 million unemployed? It is almost beyond imagining. What did those people do? What did they find to eat when there was nothing to eat? How did they heat their houses when they couldn't buy anything to heat them with? Nobody knows how people lived through those years.

It seems incredible that President Hoover wouldn't have been more effective than he was in shaping a policy which would meet this situation. But of course in his books that he wrote afterwards, he always said that he felt that it was always about to get better. Of course, he always said that prosperity was just around the corner. The more prosperous people in the community, the power-elite — a phrase that is used nowadays — all agreed that this was so. They all agreed too on his policy of not having the federal government come to the aid of individuals. Then of course when he had to run for office again and when candidate Roosevelt opposed him, he said the trouble was that everybody was afraid of what was going to happen when Roosevelt became president. He was going to punish all the businessmen, he was going to spend all the treasury's money, and he was going to do all sorts of things which scared the business community so that they wouldn't take risks. This was his theory. At any rate, this wasn't a good enough theory, and President Roosevelt not only won on it, but he set up the thing we now call the New Deal.

The economic policies were the most important policies, of course, because if you didn't establish a trend at least toward recovery — and recovery came very slowly — so that people at least felt better, and if you didn't have some public works and some relief, so that people had something to eat and so that they weren't shivering with cold through the winters, then we were on the verge of something that was simply a major disaster. Nobody knows what might have happened.

President Roosevelt used to say quite often, "What is the matter with the American people? Why do they stand it?" Yet that was the time when we never had any riots, never had any great strikes. We never had any great difficulties during all this period. That isn't the kind of time when social unrest occurs. Do you know that? Social unrest occurs when people have hope, when they see something they can get. Nobody saw anything they could get during the depression. You would have wondered really, what was the matter with the American people.

One of the things about President Roosevelt was that he did give people hope. He did give them new inspiration. You know, he saved the farmers from this disaster that was happening to them, and the very next election, they all voted against him. And this pleased him, you know. He said the American people are getting back their initiative, they are getting back their ability to fight. This was the kind of attitude he had toward what needed to be done. This was to give people new courage. And I think this is the great contribution that he made.

Recovery didn't come so very rapidly. Everybody felt better, you know, all over the country after he made that great inaugural speech [March 4, 1933] in which he said that the only thing we have to fear is fear itself. There is nothing the matter with this country. We have the ability to produce. We have the people to do the producing. Why don't we do it? We're frightened. We're frightened of nothing. People looked around and said to themselves, "This is true." They felt better. Recovery didn't come very quickly, but recovery was started in that way and was gradually built up through the years.

President Roosevelt was a much more old-fashioned person than many realized. He wanted as badly as any old-fashioned businessman to balance the budget. The budget never did get balanced in the time he was in office, but he was always talking about it. He always thought he could bring about a balance of the budget next year, and he always begrudged every cent that was spent. And yet he has the reputation of being the greatest spender of any president that we ever had. Those of us who knew him knew how this kind of thing hurt him. He was real old-fashioned about this as he was about many other things.

It was just this fact: he was willing, as he used to say, to rise above principle — which enabled him to give people this courage, give them hope, and give them the initiative to re-establish themselves in prosperity. There were a great many things which weren't economic which came from this. For instance, we stopped child labor; we stopped it dead. That was a great thing to have done. We established the social security law. Can you imagine the United States now — nobody can imagine the United States now — without a social security law. It just seems incredible that it shouldn't happen. Yet, there wasn't anything of that sort. A great many things of a similar sort happened during those years which weren't economic, which helped to give people courage and to reestablish their feeling that they could do something for themselves.

CHAPTER THREE

Is the New Deal a Square Deal?

MILO RENO

Introduction by H. ROGER GRANT

Two generations ago the American farmer found himself in deep financial trouble. Although agrarians had commonly experienced difficult times since the early post-World War I years, the crippling effect of rock-bottom prices during the early 1930s left many no profit margin. Ten cents a bushel corn, 12 cent oats, and hogs at less than one-half cent a pound destroyed the farmer's last savings and credit. In January 1933, the price index of Iowa farm products, for example, stood at the lowest point in 25 years, only 40 percent of the 1909-1914 average. Farmers understandably grew restless. A man named Milo Reno, sensitive to farmers' concerns, helped direct that unrest.

Born on a farm in southern Iowa on January 5, 1866, Reno grew up in a reform milieu. His parents expressed strong sentiments in favor of agrarian radicalism: his father backed the Granger and Greenback movements in the 1870s and early 1880s, and his father and mother both fought for populism in the 1890s. Reno, too, joined the People's Party. After attending a local Quaker academy and college, he farmed and, according to one historian, proved to be "a good farmer when he set himself to the task." More interested in politics, he became the guiding force behind the newly organized Iowa Farmer's Union in the 1920s. During that decade Reno battled for farm relief; he actively backed the McNary-Haugen bills, twice vetoed by President Calvin Coolidge.

The depression years of the 1930s brought Milo Reno his fame. In 1932 he spearheaded formation of the Farmers'

Holiday Association, an outgrowth of the older Farmer's Union. Initially the organization attracted the most depressed "dirt" farmers, but other, more prosperous, agrarians quickly joined. As support grew among farmers in the Middlewest for direct action, Reno and the Holiday Association called for a major farm strike. Members were determined to withhold their products from the marketplace to force up prices, and, more importantly, to pressure lawmakers for permanent relief. Holiday farmers became involved in a variety of militant activities — road picketing, produce dumping, stopping of sheriff's sales, etc. Although the "Holiday" failed, it gained great publicity.

With the coming of the New Deal in 1933, Milo Reno believed, as did most farmers, that agriculture had a friend in the White House. President Franklin D. Roosevelt and his Secretary of Agriculture, Henry A. Wallace (the well-known Iowa farm editor and crop scientist), quickly placed in operation the newly created Agricultural Adjustment Administration (AAA). In general, this mammoth federal undertaking was aimed at curtailing production and at bringing an immediate reduction of surpluses. After an auspicious beginning, the AAA stumbled. Commodity prices decreased in the summer of 1933, and the National Recovery Act (NRA) soon forced price increases for various goods needed by the farmer. Wrote Reno in October 1933: "We were promised a new deal. . . Instead, we have the same old stacked deck, and, so far as the Agricultural Act is concerned, the same dealers." He seemed greatly disturbed by both the highly complicated, technical details of the AAA and the controversial emergency provision of the act that permitted destruction of livestock and crops, particularly that feature which called for the slaughter of lightweight pigs and pregnant sows. (This was a move to reduce the surplus of hogs on the market, thus driving up prices.)

The airwaves provided critics of New Deal agricultural policies a means of getting their ideas to farmers and politicians alike. Reno often turned to radio station WHO ("The Voice of the Middlewest") in Des Moines, Iowa, between 1934 and his death on May 5, 1936, to explain his blueprints for better agriculture. He often demanded that the federal government guarantee the cost of production for the farmer, and he preached the old Greenback-Populist panacea of currency inflation. While some bought the Reno line, the majority of cornbelt farmers gave the Roosevelt-Wallace programs a chance. It is safe to say that by 1934 the AAA had done much to calm agrarian unrest. Of course, those who accepted the New Deal for agriculture might criticize specific features of various programs.

Reno, himself, argues one historian, "talked too much, he became a demagogue." Perhaps it is fitting that this nationally prominent Iowan backed Senator Huey Long, the Louisiana "Kingfish," and Father Charles Coughlin, the New Deal era's two great demagogues. Like both Long and Coughlin, Reno's rhetoric contained references to financial conspiracies, both international and domestic, the need for plebiscitory democracy and redistribution of wealth, and the belief that any opposition, particularly from the press, was corrupt and antisocial. Reno, Long and Coughlin, all important critics of the New Deal, thought that an aroused people could recapture the government from the selfish few who had usurped it.

In reading this typical Milo Reno radio address, broadcast May 13, 1934, note his central criticisms of the AAA. Why is he unhappy? What forces does he believe to be working against the farmer? How does he view the intellectual — "The Brain Truster" — in government? Should Reno be considered a radical, a reactionary, or something else? Does he indeed use the language of a demagogue?

The Triple A, which is that part of the New Deal affecting agriculture, has been in operation for one year. Millions have been spent, hundreds of thousands of jobs created, all of which the laborer and the farmer will, in the last analysis, be compelled to pay.

It seems to me pertinent that we take stock, as to what has been accomplished, and consider well if it has been worth while. Has it changed the general condition of agriculture for the better or the worse?

About the only argument advanced by the "Brain Busters," themselves, is that the farm income of 1933 was a billion dollars more than in the preceding year. They point with pride to this accomplishment. The thing they do not tell us is that the agricultural income in 1928 and 1929 was in excess of $12 billion and that by 1932 it had dwindled approximately five billion, and that this billion increase they boast of was more than absorbed in excessive taxation, compound interest upon the interest the farmers were unable to pay, and, under the provisions of the NRA, which advanced the prices of the things he was compelled to buy approximately 40 percent, the one-twelfth that our Brain Trusters assume was added to his price was many times absorbed and the farmers left in a more hopeless condition of debt and despair, so, taking all things into consideration, the farmer is in worse condition financially than at any time in the history of the United States, in fact, under the operation of the Triple A, he has been betrayed, bankrupted and insulted.

Dr. Raymond Moley, in the magazine *Today*, asserts that he has the evidence to prove that the United States Chamber of Commerce was responsible for the NRA, and Dr. Moley's statement is corroborated by the President of the United States Chamber of Commerce. He also stated the Triple A was conceived in the minds of 25 men, two of them professors. The others were business men and senators, who had taken an interest in the agricultural problem.

It is an admission that no farmer was consulted either in the conception or the birth of the Triple A and I maintain that no other group — labor, industry or finance — has been arbitrarily ignored and has not even been consulted as to the program or the system under which they are compelled to operate.

In selecting the heads of other departments, and in the selection of their assistants, experience and qualification was considered. In selecting a secretary of the treasury, men experienced in finance and banking were chosen. This is true of labor and of business. How different the consideration given the farmer! Instead of men of experience and judgment being selected to advise and protect the interests of the basic industry, and by far the greatest business of the nation, a group of impractical theorists, with no practical experience and whose loyalty to our form of government is, to say the least, questionable; their main accomplishment, so far, has been to take advantage of the farmer's distressed condition to coerce and intimidate him into surrendering his independence, to submit to the dictation of a group that would Russianize America.

In the face of 25 million hungry people, they have murdered five million pigs and have established a compulsory program of food destruction; in the face of 25 million half-clothed, they have destroyed our cotton. While their satellites were advising farmers' wives how to utilize used fertilizer sacks for clothing, they have paid for the destruction of cotton.

As far as possible, the Triple A has confused and disrupted real self-supporting farm organizations. Using the financial power of the federal government, it has coerced and intimidated in an effort to complete the farmers' enslavement; has refused to consider production costs as a basis for farm prices; has determined that world price shall determine the price of our farm products used in this country, which is contrary to all previous declarations made by this group. As an evidence of their intentions, when farm prices commenced to advance last July, Secretary Wallace immediately released a statement that those prices were speculative and above production costs. This statement cost the farmers hundreds of millions of dollars.

Farm prices have been held down by this group on the theory that if they advanced, farmers would refuse to accede to the Triple A program of regimentation, which is simply another name for peasantry. They have assumed unconstitutional and dictatorial powers and the right to send federal snoopers and spies on to the farms and into the homes to enforce their decrees. Under the corn-hog contract, they have demanded that the farmer waive his constitutional rights as an American citizen, the right to an appeal to the courts for equity and justice. They have decreed the farmer must suffer crucifixion, the confiscation of his home, and submit to financial ruin until he is humbled sufficiently to submit, without protest, to any burden they see fit to lay upon his shoulders. They have increased the debts of this nation — both public and private — by hundreds of millions, playing into the hands of the financial brigands that brought about, through deflation, this orgy of destruction, by multiplying the burden of debt represented in mortgages and bonds, more securely binding the laborer and the farmer to the wheels of their juggernaut, because, in the last analysis, those who toil must pay both principal and interest.

So, in summing up what the Triple A has accomplished, I assert that through bribery and coercion, it has largely broken down the morale of the self-respecting, independent farmers of America, violated both the letter and the spirit of the Constitution of the United States, taken orders from the international bankers and are attempting to destroy the peoples' confidence in representative government, and the end is not yet!

Hundreds of thousands of people in this republic, today, are asking — What next?

The threatened destructive drought prevailing at this time had caused many, who were placidly accepting the fallacies of the Brain Trust, to commence to think and ponder the situation. Many are wondering if the unthinkable crime of destroying food to relieve starvation will not bring its penalty.

I propose to give you some estimates taken from the government's monthly release, of April first, as to our real food surplus. Remember, that the food in warehouses and cold storage plants represents the difference between plenty and want. This release informs us that we have in cold storage, today for each person in the United States:

29/100 of a pound of butter;

45/100 of a pound of American cheese;

32/100 of a pound of frozen eggs, and

26/100 of one egg in the shell;

We have 81/100 of a pound of poultry;

52/100 of a pound of beef;

5 and 88/100 of a pound of pork.

The total pounds of meat per person is 6 and 96/100.

These figures are evidence that we have not to exceed one week's surplus food supply and if the people of the United States were consuming the amount of food necessary to sustain their health and mentality, we would, today, have a shortage of food instead of a surplus, and let me reiterate again, that the present deplorable situation has not been the result of over-production, but of a criminal manipulation of the nation's currency by the great banking interests interfering with the distribution of the things produced necessary to human comfort, and while President Roosevelt assured us that the money changers would be driven from the temple, would be forced to release their authority, and asked for, and was granted by Congress, the power to provide the people with a currency sufficient to efficiently transact business, the money changers have evidently had power enough — even though compelled to retreat for a time — to now move back into the temple an⸱ occupy the holy of holies; power enough to defeat every measure that has been proposed in the interests of the plain people of this nation; power enough to defeat the Frazier bill [Agrarian-radical Senator Lynn Frazier of North Dakota introduced this piece of farm relief legislation to provide farmers with the cost of production for their products. Congress, on various occasions, considered but never passed this plan.], to so emasculate silver and bonus legislation as to make them practically worthless, as far as relieving the situation is concerned; power enough to induce the president and the Secretary of Agriculture to disregard the position they occupied and the pledges they made prior to election and deny to the farmer the right to a price based on production costs, while making it a crime for other groups to sell for less.

That Wall Street is in the saddle, as far as the agricultural department is concerned, is evidenced by an Associated Press release, quoting the *Washington Post*, a paper owned by Eugene V. Meyer, who was formerly governor of the Federal Reserve Bank and has been the acknowledged enemy of all agricultural legislation, as proposing Secretary Wallace for the President of the United States in 1940. This endorsement of Wallace by one of the chief moguls of the financial interests that were to be driven from the temple is certainly evidence that the agricultural program endorsed by Secretary Wallace, is perfectly satisfactory to the Meyers, the Mellons, the Mills, the Morgans and others of their tribe [referring to former pro-business Republican Secretaries of the Treasury Andrew Mellon and Ogden Mills as well as banker J. P. Morgan, Jr.] In this *Washington Post* article, he predicates Wallace's chances for the Presidency on the supposition that he survives the scalping parties led by myself.

I wish to assure Eugene V. Meyer and the public in general that I have no desire to scalp Henry Wallace. I am only trying to remove the wig that the international bankers have placed upon his head, that has so affected his brain as to cause him to forget his commitments and his promises made before Meyer and his gang placed their wig of destruction and desolation upon his noble brow. I wish also to assure Eugene V. Meyer and his associates and the Brain Trust, that is evidently doing their bidding, that I accept as a compliment being placed in the same category as the farmer, the inflationists, and the plain people, who demand quick action.

It is all well enough for those who are not particularly

affected by the present conditions to talk about long-time programs, but to the millions of farmers and home owners who are facing the confiscation of everything they have in this world, it is quite a different matter.

Before Secretary Wallace became Secretary of Agriculture, when his own personal fortunes were affected to a great extent by the condition of agriculture, he was in the class that Eugene V. Meyer has seen fit to place myself. He demanded "quick action." I quote from his letter of January 12th, 1933:

> What is going to happen to your farm and to your neighbor's farm in the next six months? How long can you and your neighbor continue to pay taxes and meet necessary expenses at the present low price of farm products? You know the answer. So do we. That's why *Wallaces' Farmer and Iowa Homestead* has been putting all its energies into trying to get speedy action by the national congress to bring up farm produce prices. We can't afford any longer to sit back and hope for better times. Unless we know what we want and work our heads off to get it, we're licked.

The farmer's problem will not be solved by doles and subsidies, by processing taxes and regimentation. It will be solved when the farmers of this nation raise sufficient hell to compel the consideration they are entitled to and to be treated as other groups that serve society.

I am firmly convinced that the international bankers of this nation desire a change in our form of government, fully realizing that in a democracy great accumulations of wealth wrongly administered will not be permitted to survive, and there is no question but that they would much prefer a dictatorship, or fascist form of government which would permit them, by force, to enslave the people.

The American people have a momentous choice to make and I assure you that it is not far in the future. They must choose between this republic, this government of the Fathers, resting upon the Constitution of the United States, or accept a program of bureaucratic regimentation. There can be no compromise. Either our representative government will be maintained and the constitution upon which it rests be something more than a scrap of paper, or we will entirely ignore our present form and establish a new philosophy of human relationships that recognizes only power and authority sustained by military force and under which the rights of the individual are entirely destroyed. It is a sure thing that we cannot have them both, and the biggest and most important question confronting the American people at this time is whether we take our orders from the international bankers and the dictatorship of Europe, or whether we stand four-square for the principles of the Declaration of Independence, that all just governments derive their powers from the consent of the governed.

I have no sympathy whatever with the contemptible surrender, by many of our people, of those principles that have made our nation, yea, and our citizenry, great.

Clifford Berryman cartoon, April 12, 1938.   [Library of Congress
Prints and Photographs Division]

CHAPTER FOUR

The Return
of Democracy

JOUETT SHOUSE

Introduction by DAVID E. KYVIG

The American Liberty League harshly criticized the New Deal
from 1934 to 1936, and Jouett Shouse, president of the
league, was its most frequent spokesman. Shouse had long
been prominent in the Democratic Party. Born in Kentucky in
1879, he studied at the University of Missouri, worked as a
newspaperman and lawyer, and won election to Congress as a
Democrat from Kansas in 1914. A staunch supporter of
Woodrow Wilson, Shouse was defeated for reelection in 1918
and thereafter served as Assistant Secretary of the Treasury.
During the 1920s, he returned to private life, emerging briefly
in 1924 to support the candidacy of William Gibbs McAdoo
and lead the Kansas delegation to the Democratic national
convention. In 1928 Shouse campaigned for Alfred E. Smith.
After the election he was asked by Democratic National Chairman John Raskob to conduct the day-to-day affairs of the party.
From 1929 to 1932, Shouse worked tirelessly at strengthening
the Democratic organization. Traveling throughout the
country, he relentlessly attacked the Hoover administration.
The charming, eloquent, hard-working Shouse, a dapper figure
who dressed impeccably, wore a pince-nez, and carried a walking stick, bore major responsibility for successful rebuilding of
the Democratic Party in the four years after its crushing defeat
in 1928. However, since Shouse and his conservative Democratic friends, Raskob and Smith, opposed Franklin
Roosevelt's nomination for president, he was relieved of his
party position after the 1932 convention. Shouse then served
as president of the Association Against the Prohibition
Amendment until the Eighteenth Amendment was repealed in

December 1933. In August 1934, he became president of the newly-formed American Liberty League.

The Liberty League was founded by a group of men, mainly wealthy, conservative Democrats, who had become alarmed at the policies of the New Deal. Among the founders of the league were such Democrats as Raskob, Pierre and Irénée du Pont, Al Smith, John W. Davis (the 1924 presidential nominee), and former Secretary of State Bainbridge Colby. Also active were Republicans such as Representatives James W. Wadsworth of New York and James M. Beck of Pennsylvania. Most of them had participated earlier in the crusade against national prohibition, opposing that attempted reform not out of a desire to drink, rather because they regarded it as upsetting the constitutional system, dangerously expanding the power of the federal government to control individual lives, and undermining respect for all law. When the depression began, they criticized prohibition as economically harmful. Opponents of prohibition contended that the tax on liquor would permit a reduction of income taxes. The success of their fight against prohibition led them to believe they understood and represented the public interest. They distrusted Franklin Roosevelt, who had been evasive on the prohibition issue, even before he took office.

In the first months of the Roosevelt administration, business leaders, frightened by the near collapse of the economy, were reluctant to criticize any decisive actions by the government. Within a year, however, many of them had become unhappy about the extension of government authority. In the summer of 1934, the American Liberty League was founded to express that discontent. The leaders of the Liberty League regarded the New Deal as a radical departure from American traditions of individualism and limited federal government. Roosevelt, they said, was usurping the functions of the Congress and creating an omnipotent Presidency. The New Deal was subjecting American business to unprecedented control and regimentation, hampering the independence of business whose individual efforts offered the best chance for economic recovery. Roosevelt had forgotten his 1932 campaign pledge to reduce the federal budget. His extensive expenditures would create huge deficits, stimulate inflation, and require higher taxes, all of which would retard recovery. New federal programs required a huge bureaucracy which in turn could become a political weapon. Their concern led the Liberty Leaguers to spend more than a million dollars between 1934 and 1936 in an anti-New Deal publicity campaign featuring radio broadcasts, pamphlets, press releases, and speeches. During its crusade against Roosevelt's policies, the League enrolled about 125,000 members.

Franklin Roosevelt and his advisors considered the American Liberty League a real threat, especially in the winter of 1935 to 1936 when Roosevelt's popularity was at an all-time low and when Alfred E. Smith, at a dinner of 2,000 Liberty Leaguers in Washington, attracted national attention with a ringing attack on the New Deal as socialism. FDR responded in his State of the Union message, saying "We have earned the hatred of entrenched greed." The president in his 1936 re-election campaign concentrated on attacking Liberty Leaguers as "economic royalists" concerned only for themselves and their tax bills. The league was projected as a symbol of selfish wealth. When the Liberty League finally endorsed the Republican presidential nominee, Governor Alfred M. Landon of Kansas, in the fall of 1936, it shared the crushing defeat which resulted from Roosevelt's landslide reelection. Thereafter, the Liberty League faded from view, though it was not formally dissolved until 1940. Rejected and embittered, most of the Liberty Leaguers would have nothing more to do with politics.

On July 1, 1935, when the American Liberty League was attracting a great deal of attention, Jouett Shouse made a nationwide radio address on behalf of the league, berating the New Deal for the changes it had made in the American system of government. Among other things, Shouse predicted an assault by the Roosevelt administration on the Supreme Court for opposing New Deal legislation, an attack which actually took place a year and a half later as FDR sought to expand the membership of the Court to obtain a friendly majority. Shouse's statement prompts several questions. Was his emphasis on constitutionalism merely a smoke-screen for economic self-interest, or was it a sincere worry? Why would the Liberty League express such concern for the Constitution? Did, in fact, the New Deal produce significant changes in the nature of the American government? If so, were these changes for the good or the bad? In particular, was the growth of presidential power and executive bureaucracy, which Shouse described, a necessary and healthy response to the crisis of the depression or was it a dangerous centralization of authority?

I speak to you tonight as president of the American Liberty League. Our organization was formed less than a year ago. Its objectives are quite definite — to defend and uphold the Constitution of the United States, and to teach the necessity of protection of personal and property rights. Some of those inclined to be critical of our movement have urged that the Constitution was in no danger, but recent decisions of the Supreme Court make clear the facts. In the few minutes I speak tonight I shall try to show specifically how the protection to you as an individual which the Constitution provides is being threatened and the dangers to you of that situation.

In prior administrations it has been the accepted custom for the committees of Congress to write legislation, accepting or rejecting, as they might see fit, suggestions that came from the executive. Also it has been the custom that in each house there should be adequate opportunity for debate and amendment.

Under the present administration proposed bills have been prepared at the White House and not in the committees of Congress. Moreover they have been sent to Congress with orders that they should be passed without change, without the opportunity for either amendment or debate. Thus there has arisen the pernicious custom of legislating by gag rule. Under it a member of the House not only has had no opportunity to try to aid in shaping legislation, but he has not been allowed even adequately to discuss it. The excuse has been the emergency. But be not deceived. When your representatives in Congress are mere rubber stamps for an executive, no matter how worthy his motives, your rights are being destroyed and your protection under the Constitution threatened.

I recall very distinctly my service in Congress in the administration of an eminent Democratic President, Woodrow Wilson. Even in the stress of war, with the fate of the peoples of the world hanging in the balance, no attempt was made to deprive either branch of Congress of its privilege of proper consideration of legislation. Take the Draft Act, for example. Here was a proposal the importance of which could not be overestimated, which had to be passed before America could make plans for participation in the war, and yet it was debated for six full legislative days, and the debate upon it changed the attitude of the House completely and enabled the passage of the act. The Revenue Act of 1917 was considered for 11 legislative days and the Revenue Act of 1918 for 10 legislative days in the House. It should be added that none of these measures came to the floor until after an exhaustive study in the committee charged with the responsibility of fostering it.

Now let us look at some of the important legislation of the present administration. I refer only to procedure in the House of Representatives. The National Recovery Act had but two days of debate. The Agricultural Adjustment Act also but two days of debate in the House. The Federal Emergency Relief Act was debated for only two days and the Securities Act of 1933 was considered and passed in a single day. During the present session the Work Relief Appropriation Act, which wrote a blanket check to the president for $4,880,000,000 to be expended in any way he might see fit, was given only two days of discussion in the House without any prior committee consideration, and the Wagner Labor Relations Bill was passed with only one day of debate and without the opportunity for a roll call. Last week it was proposed to jam through both houses a tax measure of tremendous import with only five days time for both committee work and debate.

There is an orderly and proper method of legislating. The president is empowered by the Constitution to "give to the Congress information of the state of the Union and recommend to its consideration such measures as he shall judge necessary and expedient." The committees of Congress are supposed to weigh the president's suggestions and if approved, to frame legislation to carry them into effect. In each house there should be permitted the opportunity for debate in which any member can participate and the opportunity for the consideration of all pertinent amendments. That is the orderly way to legislate. That is the way the Congress of the United States has legislated prior to the present administration.

But latterly we have seen Congress treated with such contempt that the executive branch of the government has written the bills and has ordered Congress to pass them without change and to pass them without any opportunity for adequate debate or amendment. That is the disorderly way to legislate. It is the way of dictatorship. It is in direct contrast to every principle of democracy.

But that is not all. A few weeks ago when the Supreme Court held unconstitutional two of the pet measures of the administration and one dictatorial executive act, the president made astounding comments on the decisions. At a conference with newspaper men four days after the Supreme Court had acted he delivered a lengthy speech. At the outset he disclaimed any intention of criticizing the Court, and then for approximately an hour and a half he bitterly condemned the Court's decisions. He complained that the Court's interpretation of the interstate commerce clause meant a reversion to "horse and buggy days." He complained of the unwisdom of allowing each sovereign state to regulate its own affairs in accordance with its constitutional powers. He spoke of the need of the "restoration" to the federal government of alleged powers which it never possessed and which the Supreme Court had just stated clearly it never possessed.

The interpretation put on the president's speech by the entire press of the nation was that he contemplated an attempt to restrict the authority of the Supreme Court and thus to enlarge the powers of the executive at the expense of the judiciary. What may be his intentions in this regard only the future can disclose. It is not surprising that his plans were set back by strikingly unfavorable reaction of the country to his suggestion. However, it is notable that two members of his cabinet and an under secretary who have frequently been employed as presidential spokesmen, in highly publicized speeches since the president's blast, have made bitter attacks upon the Supreme Court decision.

Could there be more striking evidence of our need for a return to democracy?

The very antithesis of democracy is bureaucracy. Bureaucracy is a government by bureaus, a government by clerks, interference by officials vested with temporary power in the private affairs of the citizen and in the conduct of his business. Bureaucracy represents the accumulation of power in the executive branch at the expense of the legislative branch. In a broad sense the issue of bureaucracy concerns the extent to which government properly may apply its regulatory powers over the life and property of individuals. Today we are facing the menace of bureaucracy in a manner and to an extent both unparalleled and unbelievable. A democratic government is being displaced by a bureaucratic autocracy. . . .

In the realms of industry and agriculture alike this administration has attempted a policy of regimentation. It is true that the attempt in the first instance was outlawed by the Supreme

Court. Equally, it is true that eminent legal authorities hold the Agricultural Adjustment Act to be as unconstitutional as the National Industrial Recovery Act, and on practically the same grounds. [The Supreme Court declared the NRA unconstitutional in May 1935, and the AAA likewise in January 1936.] . . .

Do you realize that over a hundred thousand employees have been added to the government payroll under this administration and that every day there will be further increases? Let me cite an example of the way bureaucracy grows.

In March of 1933, Professor Tugwell appeared before the Senate committee to support the proposed Agricultural Adjustment Administration Bill. In reply to a direct question he suggested that it would not take more than 50 people in Washington to administer the bill. On April 30, 1935, according to the government's own report, there were 5,362 individuals employed in Washington alone in the administration of the AAA, apart from several thousand employed as field and county agents.

What is true here applies in multiplied other instances. Instead of attempting to curb the number of government employees the administration has given unbridled rein to every effort to increase them.

There was written at Chicago at the Democratic National Convention of 1932 the best political platform that any party has ever put forward in this country. The nominee of that convention — Governor Roosevelt — flew from Albany to Chicago in order to give immediate 100 percent endorsement, as he said, to every plank of the platform. One of the outstanding planks read as follows "We advocate immediate and drastic reduction of governmental expenditures by abolishing useless commissions and offices, consolidating departments and bureaus and eliminating extravagance, to accomplish a saving of not less than 25 percent in the cost of federal government."

In addition to his personal endorsement, Governor Roosevelt in a speech at Pittsburgh on October 19, 1932, announced that it was his intention if elected to exact a pledge from every man entering his cabinet, the first item of the pledge being "absolute loyalty to the Democratic platform and especially to its economy plank."

It is not my intention here to dwell upon the question of governmental extravagance. The ghastly record of the Roosevelt administration in its unbridled and wasteful expenditures, in its squandering of public funds for every conceivable purpose, in its total disregard of a continuance of the deficits which candidate Roosevelt so bitterly and properly condemned in connection with the Hoover administration — these form material for a speech of very real length. I am speaking now of the promise of the Democratic platform to abolish useless commissions and offices and to consolidate departments and bureaus. Instead of any attempt to achieve such result save in the first two or three months of his administration, every piece of legislation proposed or endorsed by the president has contemplated a vast increase of federal employees, a vast growth in the dangerous un-American and undemocratic authority of the appointed bureaucrats who for the moment are in absolute control of the affairs of this nation.

And yet the Democratic platform of 1932 stated, and stated truly, that "a party platform is a covenant with the people to be faithfully kept by the party when entrusted with power, and the people are entitled to know in plain words the terms of the contract to which they are asked to subscribe."

Time does not permit any detailed discussion of the president's recent so-called tax program. [On June 19, 1935, FDR proposed increased taxes on large incomes through inheritance and gift taxes and more steeply graduated individual and corporate income taxes. But the president did not fight hard for the plan as protests arose and as Congress eliminated the inheritance tax and severely reduced the graduated corporate income tax. As finally adopted, the Wealth Tax Act of 1935 did little to reduce the share of national wealth received by upper-income groups.] I merely wish to observe in passing that in no sense can it be considered a serious effort to balance the federal budget in accordance with Mr. Roosevelt's reiterated campaign promises. The estimated yield thus far suggested is about $340,000,000. To consider such a proposal as a budget balancing effort is like trying to shoot an elephant with a pop-gun. Make no mistake about it. The bill is not primarily a revenue bill. It is a political gesture pure and simple. The reckless dissipation of national resources is bound to necessitate very heavy additional taxes. But the money to meet the billions of debts which this administration is piling up will not be raised through any demagogic "Soak the Rich" or "Share Our Wealth" tax program. The bills being incurred in your name by the present administration are going to be paid by crushing taxes upon the average man and woman of this nation for many years to come.

I cannot here dwell upon other aspects of recent legislation. Suffice it to say that much of it would have suited the picture perfectly had it originated on the basis of the platform of the Socialist party rather than the platform of the Democratic party. If any experiment could be more radically socialistic or more wholly contrary to the whole basic conception of our government than the TVA, I am at a loss to imagine it. And the acts of administration of the confused medley of alphabetical agencies have veered from the extremes of fascism to the limits of socialism.

To refer once more to an out-moded but sound document, the Democratic platform of 1932 advocated "the removal of government from all fields of private enterprise except where necessary to develop public works and natural resources in the common interest." Instead of observing that dictum we have seen government literally thrust into every possible business by the present administration regardless of destruction of legitimate investments or curtailment of the rights and opportunities of citizens.

A return to democracy offers the way out. That means a return to orderly government. Why were the restrictions placed by the Constitution upon the powers of the federal government? Some would have you believe that these restrictions work to your detriment and should be removed. Why are they there? They are there simply for your protection. They guarantee your rights and privileges and opportunities. If they are taken away, if they are broken down, your liberties are in danger. No emergency can justify the assumption of arrogant power. One of the wisest of Americans, that old philosopher, Benjamin Franklin, spoke a great truth when he said: "A nation that gives up its liberty for a little temporary safety deserves neither liberty nor safety."

United Rubber Workers President Sherman Dalrymple after being beaten by anti-union thugs in Gadsden, Ala., in June 1936. At left is John House, president of the URW Goodyear local in Akron who was himself beaten up in Gadsden in 1936 and 1941. [Reprinted by permission of the United Rubber Workers.]

CHAPTER FIVE

Union Organizing in the Thirties

REX MURRAY and MRS. SHERMAN DALRYMPLE

Introduction by DANIEL NELSON

The depression and the New Deal had profound effects on American employers and workers. After 1930 employment opportunities declined precipitously, and the number of the jobless increased to more than 25 percent of the labor force by the time of Roosevelt's inauguration. Faced with insecurity and declining wages, workers first attempted to preserve their jobs and incomes. As in earlier depressions, union membership fell and strikes became less frequent. Worker militancy, at low ebb in the 1920s, all but disappeared. The New Deal economic recovery program of 1933 to 1935 had relatively little effect on profits, wages or economic opportunity (unemployment remained above 14 percent until 1941), but it had an enormous impact on the outlook and behavior of employers and workers. Practically overnight the passivity of the early 1930s ended. Encouraged by Section 7A of the National Industrial Recovery Act (1933) and the later Wagner act (1935), workers rushed to join unions and to strike when demands were not met. Employers often fought them with equal vigor, opposing their demands and their newly militant unions. As a result, the mid-1930s were years of widespread upheaval and confrontation.

Union membership statistics provide a revealing measure of these developments. Total membership nearly tripled during the 1930s from 3,600,000 to nearly 9,000,000, but the increases were highly concentrated. Transportation, mining, and construction, heavily organized before the depression, registered significant gains as unions reenlisted former members and expanded from their pre-depression bases. In manufacturing the change was even greater. Only about nine percent of American factory workers had been union members in 1930; 34 percent were union members in 1940. The greatest gains were in the mass production industries — steel, automobiles, machinery, food processing, and rubber — which had been almost completely unorganized before 1933. Most of the new members in manufacturing joined new unions, so-called industrial unions, which organized whole industries rather than crafts and which affiliated with the Committee for Industrial Organization (C.I.O.), the federation of militant industrial unions that broke from the American Federation of Labor (A.F.L.) between 1935 and 1938. However, there were significant exceptions to this pattern. Industries heavily concentrated in the South, like cotton textiles and lumber, remained largely unorganized. Even in industries with substantial organization, firms that strongly opposed unionization — like Ford, Goodyear, and the "little" steel companies — successfully combatted unions during the 1930s. Regardless of federal government policy and worker militancy, employers who were determined to avoid unions retained the upper hand.

The labor struggles that occurred in the mass production industries were among the most important and dramatic of the depression years. In part this was because so much was at stake; in part it was because employers and workers had little prior experience with union activity and therefore few standards or guidelines to follow. As a consequence they often developed new approaches to problems, methods that their counterparts in other industries later copied. A notable employer innovation, for example, was the "Mohawk Valley formula", devised by the Remington Rand Company, a New York machinery manufacturer. The "formula" was a series of prescriptions for mobilizing community resources against unions and defeating strikes. By far the best known worker innovation was the sit-down strike, which had a long history in Europe but had not been used extensively in the United States. The United Rubber Workers and United Auto Workers — industrial unions that had emerged in 1933 and 1934 — introduced the sit-down technique to the labor movement. From 1936 to 1939, when the U.S. Supreme Court ruled it illegal, the sit-down was the symbol of rank and file militancy.

The rubber industry, featured in the following documents, provides excellent illustrations of both worker militancy and employer resistance to union growth in the 1930s. From 1930 to 1933 the industry was demoralized; production and profits were low, unemployment high, and wages depressed. The Roosevelt program produced a flurry of activity, particularly in the labor relations area. Led by rank and file militants, the workers organized industrial unions and the manufacturers responded with company dominated organizations. Intense competition ensued as both types of unions sought to win the workers' favor. Although the company groups had the manufacturers' support and recognition, the independent unions gradually emerged as the dominant organizations. Most rubber workers felt that the independent unions were better able to represent their interests and sentiments, including the anti-business attitudes produced by the depression. They were also able to take dramatic, forceful actions, such as the sit-downs, to achieve their goals.

Like most industrial employees in the 1930s, the rubber workers emphasized the creation of permanent unions and the negotiation of collective bargaining contracts with their employers. To facilitate these ends, they created an international union, the United Rubber Workers, in 1935, and affiliated with the C.I.O. in 1936. But unlike some industrial unions — the United Mine Workers and the Steel Workers Organizing Committee are good examples — that placed great authority in the hands of their national officers, the U.R.W. was little more than a coordinating body in the 1930s. The locals surrendered little of their power, and the international union officials devoted much of their time to local union problems. As a result the union retained its militant, equalitarian character but probably had more difficulty than the highly centralized unions dealing with major corporations, especially the Goodyear Tire and Rubber Company, the largest employer in the industry.

As you read the documents, consider the following questions: What were the General Tire Workers grievances? What role did rank and file workers play in the sit-down strike and the Gadsden incident? What measures did General Tire and Goodyear take to combat the unions? Could the workers (unions) have been more successful by adopting different policies?

SIT DOWN — Rex Murray (1908-) was born in Ripley, West Virginia, the son of a poor farmer. He left school at 13 and worked in steel mills in the Wheeling area. Seeking better working conditions, he migrated in 1926 to Akron, Ohio, where an older sister and brother had settled during World War I. For a year he was a tire builder or assembler at the Firestone Tire and

Rubber Company. In 1928 Murray moved to General Tire, where he worked mostly in the "pit" or tire curing room. A union sympathizer since his days in the West Virginia steel mills, he was instrumental in organizing the General local in 1933 and served as local union president from 1933 to 1937. During this period he led the first sit-down strike in the industry. In 1936 Murray became an organizer for the United Rubber Workers. He remained with the international union in various capacities for 34 years. Since his retirement in 1971, he has lived on a farm near Cambridge, Ohio.

In the following account, compiled from a series of interviews with Murray in the fall of 1972, he recalls his role in the June 1934 General Tire sit-down strike.

We attempted to bargain with them [the General Tire management] as soon as we got our [AFL local union] charter in 1933. [But] they refused to recognize the union as a bargaining agency. In fact they had set up what they called an employee representation plan, which in our opinion was a company union. When we would take an issue to the company which the company felt they could grant, they wouldn't grant it to the union, but they would call a meeting of their employee representation plan. And somebody would propose the idea and the company would grant it, and then they'd post notices on all the bulletin boards throughout the plant that the employee representation plan was granted thus and so.

I would say that the working conditions in the plant was one of the main issues [making worker's unhappy] and, in fact, was as important as wages, even though we were about 17 cents an hour below the average of the Big Three. . . . We built just as many tires per man hour as they did at Goodyear, Goodrich, and Firestone; we cured as many tires, and so on and so forth . . . so we felt we was entitled to at least equal pay.

[By the spring of 1934 it was apparent that the company would not bargain or satisfy the workers' other demands unless forced to do so, and Murray and the other local leaders began preparations for a strike. The company still refused to negotiate or to make concessions, and the local leaders found themselves] in almost constant conflict with the management . . . until the strike actually took place in mid-June.

There was pressure brought to bear on us [by Coleman

Claherty, the A.F.L. organizer assigned to the rubber industry] to wait and give one of the Big Three the opportunity to go forward. At that time I had to inform [Claherty] that I didn't think that [we] could indefinitely collect dues from people who could not gain recognition and the right to bargain for wages, hours, and working conditions. . . . There was no assurance that three months from now, six months from now, one of these others [would] be in a position to do it. . . . The people was becoming dissatisfied and discouraged with the progress that was being made. And they took the position of either get recognition or force the issue, one of the two.

We checked what had happened in the rubber and other mass industries and how the companies had forced them to strike for recognition and then immediately go for a court injunction to prevent picketing or a very limited number of pickets if they were admitted at all. And they would insist that the law enforcement officials carry out the mandate of the injunction. And if necessary, they would come in and bust a few heads and bust up the picket line, and there was your labor organization, gone up the river. We [also] talked to people who had first hand knowledge of what had happened in previous attempts to organize.

[During these discussions Murray suggested the idea of occupying the plant.] They thought I was off my rocker. Claherty in particular said I was crazy. I said to him, with all due respect, "Sir, if you can find another method that will work and be effective and establish collective bargaining, I can assure you that the vast majority of the people in the plant will be back of you and support you." [But] he didn't have no other methods, no other procedures. He'd exhausted all he knew.

[Local union officials] were in favor of it. They couldn't find a better method or a better procedure to follow, so they agreed with attempting to go this route. We [then] started a program of exchanging information with our key people — committeemen and officers in the plant — and we run a "school" for a couple of weeks trying to anticipate what actions or what the company may try to do and try to build a counter offensive to offset it if it became necessary. I say "school" — the group got together; we discussed it, we discussed the strategy and worked it out on that basis.

For example, if they brought the police in and it got to the point where we felt it was necessary . . . we could give them [the strikers] a signal and they would go to work, and they would work until the police left the plant and then we would shut it down again. This was the plan. And if we got . . . [arrested] inside the plant, it would be no different from insisting on our rights to picket outside the plant and being arrested outside the plant and being taken and thrown in jail. So this was a chance we had to take. . . . We discussed the thing in detail from A to Z and tried to anticipate what action the company might take and what our counteraction might be.

The stewards were pretty well informed to keep [these plans] . . . under their hat and at the proper, opportune time these people would be given a signal what to do or what not to do. They explained to the rest of the people that a signal was to be given. It wasn't to be done unless the signal was given. [But the rank and file] was ready for whatever action was necessary to establish recognition, sit-down, walkout, or whatever. They'd go either way. We was going to try the sit-down method, and if that didn't work, we would discuss it further and decide what further course of action to pursue. [A degree of flexibility was also necessary because of the presence of numerous spies in the union, including one member of the bargaining committee.]

[One particular problem confronting the local leaders was the presence of women in many of the departments who would presumably occupy the plant with the male employees.] We anticipated a certain amount of criticism. But on the other hand, we couldn't ask the females to stay home and the males to come to work . . . the females wanted to be part of the activity, part of the action.

What triggered the thing was that they cut the rates in the truck tire department. This became a real hot issue . . . we were ready for a hot issue anyway, but this was the breaking point. After we gave them an ultimatum — called a meeting at the [East High] school auditorium [June 17], took a vote, and the membership authorized the officers of the local to give them 24 hours to correct it or else. And we served the notice on them, and they didn't move so we put the sit-down into effect. We served notice on them on Monday [June 18] and Tuesday evening . . . they claimed that [Mr. William] O'Neil, the president of the company, was out of town, and we should give him an opportunity to be in on the discussion and the meeting. And we said, if Mr. O'Neil was interested, he could be here. We felt this was as important as anything else he might have to take up his time. . . . And we told them we'd given them two hours additional time, and that's what we gave them. . . . We said we would take whatever action necessary . . . I don't remember if we said we would strike or sit-down or what. But anyway we served the notice: either restore the piece-work rates or else.

I think they . . . [wanted us to strike] because they wanted a chance to bust it up. And that would have been the opportunity, but they didn't get it. [The strike] started when I walked through the plant and gave [the workers] the signal to shut it down. That's when it started. And as fast as I could walk from one department to another, throughout the plant, that's when it went down. And one of the plant guards was following me from about the time I got to the second department, telling me I couldn't do it. "You have to stay in your own department." I said, "I'll go back to my department in a little while!" and I just kept walking, one floor to the other. When I gave them the signal, they pulled the switches and shut it down.

They just stayed there, and they changed shifts, just like they was working. People who come to work next shift came right in the plant, sit down beside the machine. Those people went home and the next shift, right around the clock.

There was one guy that continued to work. I went to the foreman . . . and said there was one individual who apparently did not want to cooperate with the rest of the people. And to prevent trouble I would appreciate if he would say a good word to this individual. And the general foreman went to him and what he said I don't know but the machine shut down. [The other workers] played checkers, played cards, and things of this nature. Mostly just sitting around — bull session.

[The management] was confused and . . . didn't know what to do . . . . Mr. [Charles] Jahant, who was vice-president in charge of manufacturing at the time . . . made a request that he be permitted to talk to the people, and we said we'd cooperate with him, and he would talk to the people if he wanted to, but there'd be no vote taken. And he went through the plant, department by department, and the people listened to what he had to say and sat tight. And later he wanted all of them together, and we arranged to have all the people who was off shift . . . come into the plant, and we had a meeting in the back of

the plant, in a lot. People just stood up and he used the platform, the loading platform for the railroad cars. . . . And when
we got through talking he tried to take a vote there and I
stopped him. I told him there'd be no vote. In fact he even
come right out and said "Will those in favor of returning to
work move to the right and those that wished to continue the
strike move to the left" and I stepped in and interrupted him
. . . and said there will be no vote taken.

And then we marched out of there. We went directly from
there to the East High School auditorium to hold our meeting.
. . . And this is when . . . [the strikers] voted to establish a
picket line in place of the sit-down in the plant. And we
changed it from a sit-down strike to a . . . [conventional strike]
outside the plant . . . . The people thought they would have a
lot more freedom and it would eliminate considerable criticism
that was developing because of the males and females both
being in the plant, sitting down.

I think they [the management] was confused and sur-
prised that the people would strike together the way they did
and support the union and . . . was afraid . . . [an effort to expel
the strikers] would create some kind of destruction of property
in the plant or violence and people getting hurt, and they didn't
want to become involved in it. And perhaps there was one
[other] point. . . . They thought if they let . . . [the workers
strike] for a few weeks and cool their heels that they'd change
their mind and be willing to crawl back to work on their hands
and knees. . . . [But] this sit-down established a tremendous
amount of confidence in the people . . . and . . . they would
stick together and if necessary fight to win their ends.

The General Tire strike continued for more than a month. At
first the company refused further contact with the union.
When the management sponsored a back-to-work rally on July
10, the strikers marched to the meeting site, took over the
platform, and declared their determination to stay out until
their demands were met. A few days later General re-opened
negotiations, and on July 18 agreed to a nine-point memorandum, conceding, in effect, the strikers' demands. Thereafter
management would meet with the workers' representatives,
pay rates comparable to those paid in the Big Three plants,
consider seniority in making job assignments, improve working

conditions in the plant, and abolish the employee representation plan. While the union did not gain formal recognition, it
had won a significant victory. Workers in the other Akron
plants, moreover, had learned that with the right approach,
they too could "win their ends."

PEACE TO VIOLENCE — Sherman Dalymple (1889-1962),
like Murray, was born and raised on a West Virginia farm.
After three years in the West Virginia oil fields, he moved to
Akron in 1914 and worked at the B.F. Goodrich Company for
several years. In 1917 Dalrymple enlisted in the Marines and
served with distinction in France. Returning to Goodrich in
1919, he worked there, mostly as a tire builder, until 1935.
With the passage of section 7A, he helped organize the
Goodrich workers and was elected local union president. In
1935 he became the first president of the international union.
Enormously popular with the rank and file for his honesty,
unpretentiousness and personal courage, he guided the U.R.W.
during its formative years. After ill health forced him to resign
the union presidency in 1945, he served as treasurer of the
C.I.O. Southern Organizing Committee. Dalrymple retired to
California in the 1950s and died there in 1962.

In February 1936, workers at Goodyear used the sit down
to win a dramatic victory at the Akron plant, a victory that
initiated what Harold Roberts, the first historian of the union,
called the "great stall." For nearly six years the union was
unable to obtain recognition or a collective bargaining contract
from Goodyear. In Akron, where the U.R.W. represented a
majority of the Goodyear employees, it engaged in endless,
fruitless negotiations. In other communities, where the union
was weaker, it encountered other forms of resistance. In
Gadsden, Alabama, a stronghold of anti-union sentiment, the
U.R.W. had few members. Union men were often discharged or
discriminated against. Finally, in June 1936, U.R.W. President
Dalrymple visited Gadsden to call attention to the company's
policies and bolster the morale of the local members. Mrs.
Dalrymple, who accompanied him, recalls in this statement,
prepared for a legal suit against Goodyear, their experiences
when Dalrymple attempted to speak to a crowd of anti-union
hecklers and thugs.

The meeting was called to order and Mr. Gray introduced Mr.
Green from the Central Labor Union. He spoke about 10

minutes, I imagine, and the boys booed and carried on quite a bit, and then they settled down again. Then Mr. Gray introduced Sherman, and the boys just booed and carried on, yelling "who the hell sent for him," and he tried to explain and tried to get them quiet. But they just wouldn't listen, and then they started throwing rocks and eggs, and Sherman asked them to please be seated, but they wouldn't do it so in came the sheriff and his deputies. The sheriff said, "Now, Dalrymple, you might as well break up your meeting, and Sherman said he would. When the sheriff came in with the deputies, the squad men from Goodyear all stood up and told them who to search, and they searched all union men but did not pay any attention to the others, and then the sheriff told the cops to take the union men out the front way, which they did, and he said, "Come on, Dalrymple, go with me." He took him by the arm and took him out the back way with all that bunch of Goodyear men and as soon as they got outside they started beating him.

There was a man on each side of him who took his wrists and pulled his hands clear up in the back of his neck, and I could just hear his shoulders give, and then two men got him by the hair and pulled his head back, and then they just held him there and let the men beat him on the head, face, and in the eyes. They choked the breath out of him twice. He said he thought he was gone.

Then he managed to get over in front of the hotel, and they started beating him again, and all the time the sheriff was just walking along behind, and all he said was, "Boys, don't do that, don't do that." But he never raised a hand to help Sherman in any way. He got up close to the screen door, and it is that big heavy wire and he got his fingers caught in that. He ripped the screen clear off the door and yet they got him out on the sidewalk and started beating him. I was pleading with them to let him go, and I don't know how he got away from them to get to the hotel, but he finally got to the hotel and the sheriff came right with us and all those men and Sherman said to the sheriff, "Now, sheriff, I should have medical attention, I am in a very bad condition." The sheriff, said, "Dalrymple, the whole city is up in arms against you, and I won't be responsible for a thing that happens to you." I said to the sheriff, "Let a man be beat up in this condition, and you won't even let me have medical attention for him." And then there were about four or five of those great big husky fellows got up in my face and said, "Now God Damn you, if you want him now, you had better take him out of here." And they warned me not to let the sun shine on him again in Gadsden, and so we checked out of the hotel.

I begged the sheriff to give us protection until we got out of the city, and he refused that and, of course, my husband's eyes were in such a shape that he couldn't see to help me, and we just drove up one street and down another for quite awhile until we got out of Gadsden. And then I drove about 30 miles to Collinsville, Alabama, and I stopped at a tourist camp there, and there was an old gentlemen, and he was kind enough to direct us to a doctor. We got the doctor out of bed, and he came back down to his office, and as he looked at my husband he said, "Where did you bring this man from?" And I said "Gadsden," and he asked me if I realized his condition, and I said, "Yes, I do, but he doesn't." He said, "This man has lost enough blood to kill him let alone the injuries he has," and he begged Sherman to let him take him to a little doctor that he knew would take care of him. But Sherman said, "No" that he had to get to Akron. The doctor saw that he was going on so he put some shots in his nose, eyes and mouth to clot the blood so that he wouldn't bleed so much, and he fixed me some ice bags to put on his head when we stopped.

I drove then about 130 miles before I stopped that night, and I got him into a tourist camp and put the ice on him, but he didn't rest any. We had only been in bed a couple of hours, when he turned over and laid his arm on me and said, "Oh, mom, please let's go to Akron." So I got him dressed at once, and I drove 480 miles to my sister's place at Blanchester, Ohio, about six o'clock in the evening, and my sister insisted upon him having her doctor there. But he wouldn't, and he wouldn't even let me send a telegram into Akron, Ohio, so I begged him to let me telephone Frank Grillo, which he did, and he warned Frank that he wasn't to tell anyone in Akron. So we stayed at my sister's that night and left there at five o'clock the next morning and got into Akron about 11 o'clock and he called Frank then and told him who he wanted him to bring out and he gave his story to the boys just as he had been beaten up and the photographers took his picture and I believe the last of the boys left about six o'clock that evening.

He started into the house. I told him to come in, that I had dinner ready and he just got inside the door and went to lie on the davenport, but he couldn't make it and fell across the end of the davenport. I said, "Sherman, you see what you have done, if you had only gone to bed when we got home." He said, "Now, mom, there is nothing to worry about. If I die now, it won't make any difference. I explained everything to the boys, and I know they won't leave a stone unturned." And from that time on, he didn't seem to care.

That night he tumbled and tossed all night and had awful spells. He would grab me and say, "Oh, mom, I wish you would quit doing that, you just scare me to death." And after he got over it he said, "My, oh my, is my head causing me all of this." I tried all night to get a doctor, until five o'clock Tuesday morning. I got one, and just as soon as he came he said my husband was in a very bad condition. He couldn't tell exactly whether it was concussion. He gave him a shot and said he would be able to tell by 12, so he came back at 12 and told me to get my husband ready for the hospital immediately, which I did, and they took him to the hospital in an ambulance at two o'clock.

They took x-ray pictures that evening which showed him having hemorrhages and also slight concussion and fractures.

On Wednesday morning the doctor told me he thought he had passed the crisis, and then Thursday morning he was sure he had, and he said that unless something else set in, he was sure he would get well.

The Goodyear strategy was successful for several years. In Akron and other union towns, the company's delaying tactics postponed union recognition until 1941, making Goodyear one of the last major mass production manufacturers to agree to a union contract. (The other major rubber manufacturers capitulated earlier — Firestone in 1937, B. F. Goodrich and U.S. Rubber in 1938, and General Tire, which had dealt informally with the union since 1934, in 1939.) In Gadsden, the Goodyear version of the Mohawk Valley formula prevented union organizers from making inroads until World War II. Local men who joined the U.R.W. often lost their jobs; organizers who came after Dalrymple received a similar welcome. Finally, in 1942, pressured by the federal government, Goodyear recognized the U.R.W. in Gadsden.

The Elmer Powers family on their Boone County, Iowa, farm in the early 1930s Elmer, the diary-keeper, is second from the left. Also shown are his son and daughter, his wife, Minnie and on the left, a city relative who was a factory worker. [Reprinted by permission of H. Roger Grant and L. Edward Purcell, Years of Struggle: The Farm Diary of Elmer G. Powers, 1931-1936. (Ames: Iowa State University Press, 1976.)]

CHAPTER SIX

Day by Day on the Farm, 1937

ELMER G. POWERS

Introduction by
H. ROGER GRANT and L. EDWARD PURCELL

The daily diary kept by Elmer Gilbert Powers (1886-1942) during the New Deal era is a remarkable document. An articulate and sensitive Boone County, Iowa, farmer, Powers wrote his "Day-by-Day on the Farm" account for the region's premier farm publication, *Wallaces' Farmer.* Although he often typed several hundreds words each day, little of the diary appeared in print.

Living on rich central Iowa land, perhaps some of the best in the world, Powers experienced numerous difficulties during the 30s. He had to cope with meager depression prices for his products; he endured the complexities of New Deal agricultural programs; he battled the capricious forces of nature — severe winters and prolonged drought. On several occasions Powers came uncomfortably close to losing his 160-acre farm; yet he held on through these years of struggle.

Politically, Powers supported the Republicans; his family and most of his neighbors also were staunch members of the Grand Old Party. But as economic conditions worsened in the early 1930s, Powers and others began to rethink their political positions. Although he never voted for Franklin D. Roosevelt (a blizzard kept him from the polls in 1932, and he backed Governor Alf Landon in 1936 and Wendell Wilkie in 1940), Powers enthusiastically supported the appointment of Democrat Henry A. Wallace ("editor of our favorite farm paper") as Roosevelt's Secretary of Agriculture. Throughout the New

Deal years cornbelt farmers frequently turned from the Republican column to the Democratic column.

When the Farmers' Holiday movement erupted, Powers expressed sympathy with its over-all goal to improve the farmers' lot. But he never endorsed Milo Reno's crusade. Rather, Powers joined countless other farmers who either wholeheartedly backed the "New Deal" for agriculture or were willing to give it a try. For Powers and the typical farmer, it was not always easy. Drought in 1934, again in 1935, and especially in 1936 prompted much criticism of the AAA's surplus-reducing features. These dry years understandably reduced surpluses, and although prices subsequently rose for farm commodities, many farmers, including Powers, had little to sell.

Powers' statements in his 1937 diary reveal that the Roosevelt administration by that time had not solved all the farmer's problems. Yet, the New Dealers had not abandoned their efforts. When the Supreme Court on January 6, 1936, ruled portions of the AAA unconstitutional, Congress, pushed by Secretary Wallace, passed on February 29 the Soil Conservation and Domestic Allotment Act, a substitute for the "first" AAA. Under the guise of soil conservation, the new law's main objective was to raise the level of per capita farm income. The measure offered farmers cash bounties for planting soil-enriching grasses and legumes instead of soil-depleting commercial crops. Farmers were to be paid from congressional appropriations, not from taxes on food processors (the High Court had opposed that feature of the AAA). The new act also was aimed at a long term solution to price imbalance through conservation, a lesson learned from the drought years. Later the Agricultural Adjustment Act of 1938 marked the third and final stage of the New Deal's agricultural program. New Dealers argued that this measure occupied a middle position between the AAA of 1933 and the Soil Conservation and Domestic Allotment Act of 1936, since it contained elements of both laws.

In this edited version of the Powers diary, note the daily problems encountered by a typical Iowa farmer. Also consider these questions: What changes in technology occured during this period? Were such changes for the better? How did Powers feel about organized labor? Similarly, what were his feelings toward "relief" workers? And why? What impression did the New Deal programs have on him? Finally, what impact did hard times have on Powers and his community?

Sat., Jan. 2. 37.
All kinds of weather today. Damp and misty this morning, colder before noon and a fair sort of blizzard this afternoon. Went to town this afternoon. Baler parts were finished so I could get them, and we needed groceries and lamp gasoline. Some of the town folks are beginning to use kerosene lamps. They complain about the cost of electricity. This town is on the edge of the drought belt and business isn't any too good.

Sun., Jan. 3. 37.
I have been trying to keep an especially close watch on several farmers, who for various reasons were compelled to have closing out sales and moved to town. They are having much trouble to find any kind of work to do. This is very bad. They are accustomed to many things to keep them busy. And they are not pleased to be drawing on their small reserve capital to live on while they are not working.

Thur., Jan. 7. 37.
Grain and livestock markets are holding their own, with slight advances in one or two items. Many farmers that I talk to are quite disgusted with the striking automobile workers. Of course, we do not know so much about working conditions, but we are rather of the opinion that if our products could be handled more directly to them, their dollar would buy more for them. There are too many middlemen taking toll from the producer to the consumer.

Sat., Jan. 9. 37.
The weather moderated somewhat, and we went to town this afternoon. Quite a number of folks in town this afternoon. I have two notes due at the bank, but they were very busy, and I will go back next week.

To me, the most noticable thing along the way to town was the empty and near empty corn cribs on the farms we passed. Recently, I have heard a number of farmers say that whatever happens they will never burn any corn again. [As part of the surplus-reduction features of the first AAA, participating farmers were paid in 1933 to destroy portions of their crops and livestock. In subsequent years, the AAA provided financial incentives to limit farm production.] It is only several years ago that this was rather an extensive practice.

Tue., Jan. 12. 37.

This afternoon I went to town, to see the banker. I paid up the interest and a small amount on the principal, and the banker very generously extended the notes until next December. At this time the young cattle should bring enough to clear up the whole amount. And is it a relief to me. Things looked much better to me here at the place this evening. Of course there is a number of things to annoy me yet, but with these notes a long way ahead I can find a way to work out the coming Land Bank payments. [In order to save his farm, Elmer Powers applied to the Federal Land Bank (part of the Farm Credit Administration) for a mortgage-relief loan. The purpose of the Land Bank was to provide easy, long-term credit for farm owners so they could retain ownership during the depression.] And I am sure that we are situated much better than many others. I never give a thot to those who had rain and good crops, with good prices. My sympathy is all with the others.

Thur., Jan. 14. 37.

As I had looked for, we enjoyed clear weather today. But it was very cold. As there is quite a lot of wood around the place that should be cleaned up and I do not seem to have time for everything that I wish to do, I drove to the village, planning to find someone to cut the wood on shares. But I did not succeed. Everyone is working on P.W.A., about 15 miles from town. They work four days one week and three the next. I was told they receive more than $3 per day of six hours. I understand all of these men were employed as railroad section men [railroad laborers] for the full section year last year. Until recent years railroad section men did not require this assistance. At each house I called at I had difficulty in arousing anyone because of the loud radios that were turned on. Perhaps all of these things will work out alright. I hope so. But I know many farm families whose incomes the past year did not equal a section laborer, and whose income during this winter is so small that it can hardly be mentioned. And no one thinks of any relief or assistance for them.

Fri., Jan. 15. 37.

Our township held a meeting and elected committeemen for the soil conservation work [to implement the Soil Conservation and

Domestic Allotment Act] for the coming season. The old township board was reelected. Two visiting county officers conducted the meeting and about 30 farmers were in attendance,
with 25 voting. When we started in the old corn-hog work
[under the first AAA in 1934], more than 100 attended this
township meeting. We have around 130 farms in the township.
Of course some will work with the plan, who were not in attendance at the meeting. But I do not look for many to, as the
situation looks now. Farmers in attendance at this meeting
seemed to be much more interested in a proposed electric light
and power line around the township.

Thur., Jan. 21. 37.

We experienced unusually mean weather today. Cloudy and
cold, an intense cold. We did not do anymore outside work than
was necessary. About the middle of the afternoon Hub Clark
phoned that a general meeting, about a R.E.A. [Rural Electrification Administration] light line would be held this evening, in
the high school building, in town and for me to come and to let
as many neighboring farmers as I could, know about it. So I did
some phoning around the community.

About 75 farmers, from four townships were in attendance
and a speaker explained about the R.E.A. projects and how
they were handled. A committee of five men, one from each of
the four townships and a general chairman, were elected to
carry on the further work.

Thur., Jan. 28. 37.

In town this evening I met a salesman who says that he sold
four new spreaders today. In the northeastern part of the state
[where rainfall was adequate during the 1930s]. Then he began
telling about the drought areas he has been in recently, and how
difficult things were there for some of the farm folks. He was
much affected by some of the things he had learned and his
voice was rather shaky as he had difficulty in controlling his
emotions. He suggested that we did not visit some places.

Fri., Jan. 29. 37.

Our R.E.A. project held another meeting tonight. The place of
meeting this time was in the Legion Dugout, and this meeting
was well attended. A pleasant, instructive speaker made it a

profitable meeting. A sign up of line customers will, I think, be the next step.

Secretary [Henry] Wallace was in and around Des Moines today and I would have liked very much to have gone in to the city and met him again, but I think it is very necessary that work on the proposed light line be rushed before farmers get into the fields this spring.

Wed., Feb. 3. 37.

We have a change in our county administration, I think all new men on the Board of Supervisors, and so far this season the snow plow has passed our farm only one time. It is possible that the plows are routed differently this season, and that it may work out more efficiently, but up till now it has not. Our mail carrier continues to get over part of his route. However, this is not so much a factor in farm life anymore, because of the radio. We can get the news, while it is new that way and not wait for the paper. With the coming of television, or something similiar, so that we get radio pictures, I think will come the passing of newspapers.

Sat., Feb. 6. 37.

Frank Staebler came and cut some wood and helped with the sawing and took a load of blocks home with him. Neither he or I ever worked in an automobile factory, but we agree that the strike is a money losing proposition for the laborers. Of course it is for the owners too, but perhaps they can stand it a little better than the laborers. Frank and I think a short-time strike, to draw the attention of the public and then a resumption of work might be a better plan.

In our own line of business we are disgusted with the Department of Agriculture for importing eggs and then when the price is on the skids, buying up eggs and giving them away in an effort to correct the price.

Mon., Feb. 15. 37.

I had to do something today, about raising money for the Land Bank payment and about the only thing I could do was to sell some of the corn. Perhaps I can reduce livestock feed and change methods and get along with less corn. I had hoped to be able to bale and sell straw and hay for about half of the payment. I could not find any farmer feeders who would buy corn at this time. The elevator would pay $1.10 for shelled corn and $1.06 for ear corn. The road is drifted with snow and I could not get the sheller here to the place. So I sold the corn in the ear, and hauled it myself. I hauled one load this forenoon, and three this afternoon. The weather was bad this afternoon. Almost a regular blizzard, but I continued to haul because I was afraid the road might fill up. Must haul two more loads tomorrow.

Tue., Feb. 16. 37.

Contrary to what I expected the weather was clear today, and I hauled two more loads of ear corn this forenoon. I just cannot spare anymore corn and must get the remainder of the loan money from some [other] source. I needed $340 and the around 260 bu. of corn made around $270. I paid my account at the elevator and mailed a check for $260 to the Land Bank. The rest will have to come a little later.

Thur., Feb. 18. 37.

We did not do much baling today. Only 10 bales this forenoon. The party I had written to several days ago came this forenoon and bot the straw at $7 per ton and the hay at $14 per ton. He is to take it from the place. He comes from Denison, Iowa [a community hard hit by drought in 1936]. We are to bale the remainder as soon as convenient.

This afternoon I took our male hog to the community sale. It is rather late in the season to sell male hogs, but I wished to be sure we were thru with him. I had paid $14.25 for him the 13th of last November and I received $12.50 for him today.

Wed., Mar. 3. 37.

I drove to the county seat this morning and finished up the Land Bank payment. It had taken much time and effort to do this. I hope this season that I will have a normal crop and get an average price for it and that the further payments will not be so difficult.

This afternoon I was in town again and traded the old car for another used one. The old one was doing fairly good and might have gotten along with for some little time yet, but it would have cost quite a lot for repairs. The used one I am buying will seem quite an improvement for us. Both the old and the used one we are buying are Fords.

Fri., Mar. 5. 37.

I saw a Boone County farmer today who could not borrow a hundred dollars without giving a mortgage on all of his personal property. He has a quarter section farm, adjoining the pavement and does not have what is considered a heavy mortgage on it. I still hear of communities where farmers are going broke by the dozens and apparently nothing is being done to help them.

Thur., Mar. 18. 37.

Frank Staebler and I went to the sale today. He received some of his Soil Conservation money last week. [Farmers frequently referred to the cash payments they received for signing-up under the Soil Conservation and Domestic Allotment Act as "soil conservation money."] He has not had a hog of any kind on his place for a long time, and today he bot a white brood sow. He needs another horse, but his S.C. money won't reach only so far.

I had used my S.C. money to pay taxes with, and being out of money, I sold two calves. Then I bot one smaller one.

Wherever farmers meet I frequently hear the statement made that "I hope this will be a good crop year this year."

Mon., Mar. 22. 37.

There continues to be many disturbing factors in the farming situation. The advancing grain market that is making millions for South American farmers is one of them. Or perhaps it isn't millions, and perhaps it is speculators and not farmers that is making it. But one fact persists and that is that if the American farmers and business men, I mean by American - the United States, would have more intelligently handled the crop situation, it would have been our producers who would have made this money.

Tue., Mar. 30. 37.

Today was the sign up day for our part of the township, on the soil conservation program. The committeemen were at the town hall, in the village. Not many farmers were there while I was there, either this morning or this afternoon. It seems that, locally at least, the sign up will be very light this year. There have been so many mistakes made, the checks have been so slow coming and no provision was made to care for anyone if we should have a crop failure as we had last year. I signed up and hope my payments will be enough to meet the taxes and that I will get my check next fall, in time to pay them with it.

Fri., Apr. 2. 37.

We went to town this afternoon. It was pretty sloppy to try to do anything around the place. In town I went to the hatchery, to the box factory for egg cases, and to the cold storage plant for more of our frozen beef. Then I went to the court house to see what my taxes would be, those I must pay this year. I wondered if my Soil Conservation payment would pay them. I learned that there would be an increase of perhaps $30 to $40 over last year. Taxpayers seem helpless to protect themselves. The government seems to be determined to make the business men and property owners work longer and harder days and take it away from them in taxes to pay to other folks who will not be bothered with a business or owning property.

I met a man today who has been doing some work on a tenants owning farms proposition, and he confidentially told me that tenants did not want to own farms. Why should they? They were escaping all the bother and worry of improvement, taxes, etc.

Sun., Apr. 4. 37.

I made a little drive today. Not far. Just far enough to get over into the more serious drought country of last summer. There are still many signs of this drought. The effects of it will continue for a long time. There are many scars on the landscape. The spindly stalks of corn in the stalk fields and the short, small shocks of fodder. The new seeding that did not come and the older pastures and meadows that were killed by the heat and lack of moisture. The odd, irregular furrows that were plowed thru meadows and pastures to head off fires and the many stubbs of fence posts, where posts had burned. Many farm buildings need painting and repairing and some of it at least could have been done, but for the drought.

But after all these are small things, because it is the effect on the people that is the most serious. Many homes have been broken up. Separations and divorces. Many cases of illness. More insanity, more unmarried mothers, more young people scattered from the farms, more discouragement etc., than at any time I can remember of.

Tue., Apr. 6. 37.

A neighbor, I will not mention his name, asked me to haul stock for him today. He sold a cow and a hog. I took them to the packing plant. He went along. On the road I asked him, how come, because I could see he needed them at home. He said to buy gas and oil for the tractor. Seed oats, seed corn, feed baby chicks etc. He mentioned several hundred dollars worth of things he should buy, and at the plant he received $67 for the two of them.

At the plant it was the same story. Old model trucks and trailers behind cars, with one cow, often a partly dry milk cow, a hog or two or a calf. But mostly the same as my neighbor, one of the cows and one of the hogs were going, that the business may be kept going a little longer or that the crops might be put in. Always not nearly enough money received to anywhere near do the job.

And our state legislature dilly dallying around. Our leading daily paper doing nothing and our leading farm paper aiming way over our heads with ideas that may or may not help at some future time.

Fri., Apr. 9. 37.

Looking around the countryside, from my fields I can see many changes in it. But the changes I was thinking about today were the changes in farm ownership. Across the road west of me is owned by a publisher of some sort of a set of books. They were sold mainly to rural school teachers. This publisher has been tangled with the law several times. South of me is owned by a grain dealer, said to have made more than $150,000 in corn trading last summer. East of him is owned by the owner of a flour mill. And the surrounding farms are all distant owned. I do not have an owner operator for a neighbor. I wish I did. These tenant farmers neighbors are alright in a way, but they cannot take the place of owners for neighbors.

Week of May 1 to 7., 37.

Here at our place our young stock losses have been heavy in spite of anything I could do. The banker has [been] quite lenient. D.L. [Powers's son] has a goodly lot of young poults, but the poultry business is still terribly mixed up, as has been the cream business. Men, truck drivers, actually have fist fights about the little bit of cream we farmers are producing. They all want to haul it and there isn't enough to make it profitable for one.

Week of Sun., May 23 to Mon. May 31. 37.

The rush of farm life continues. Planting nearly all done. Except for where heavy rains have damaged the fields. Some farmers have finished the first cultivation. Soy beans all seeded on some farms. Markets continue good. Feed situation acute. New and used tractors still going out. Final payments of Soil Conservation grants to many farmers were made this week. They run from a few cents to $50. Ours was $33.40.

Tue., June 1. 37.

I finally bot a tractor today. A used Farmall. It has been reconditioned and painted. A neighbor has been using it for cultivating the past few days, while he was waiting for the new one he had ordered. The dealer had furnished it to him. I traded one of my old tractors, several of the older horses etc. I do not know how I will make out without horses for most of the work. But I am thinking about the corn crop I would like to raise this year and the way I want to get the work done and it seems that the later tractor may be the way out. Nearly all of the neighbors have tractors for cultivating and I have waited a long time for a more modern tractor. The cultivator that I got in the trade is not a new one, but I will get along with it I am sure.

Wed., June 2. 37.

This afternoon we mowed the lawn and various odd jobs. Late this evening a stock truck picked up the horses I traded on the tractor deal. I remarked that this was the first time in years that horses left my place alive. Usually the dead animal truck hauls away any horses that leave this place.

Week ending Sat., June 19. 37.

Another busy farm week is history. Some oats fields, neutral ground, is being clipped. With nearly all of the grain bins and corn cribs empty, this is rather a hard thing for many farmers to do. But they all know what a calamity very low prices can be. The weather, in our community, has been very good. Several afternoons were exceedingly warm, for the work horses. The early haying is all completed. Corn is a fair stand and making good progress. However, those communities that have been visited by heavy rains and hail storms, are finding their corn fields rather hard to take care of. Altogether, over the corn belt, I would say that corn prospects, at this time, are only fair, hardly that.

Grain, for feed, continues to be the major problem. Farm help is annoying. Day wages are too high and men are hard to find.

Week of July 24 to 31. 37.

This week is the opening threshing week in our community. There is only one steam rig in operation. All others are tractor power. And they run to rather smaller outfits. Fewer hired men are at work, and many crews are rather short handed. The crop of straw is heavier than the average crop and the grain yield is better than usual, with fair quality. However, it is expected that much of the greater yield will be fed to livestock and poultry before the corn husking season begins, because stocks of corn, on the farms, are very low, and on many farms, not at all. Much of the oats crop is going to market, because of small storage room on the farms. The price has declined to 20 to 22 cents per bu. There is some talk of reviving the old warehouse loan plan. Farmers are very bitter toward any and all persons and factors who many have had any connection with present low price situation. They feel that the good crop they have produced is much needed, is not in excess of what will be required for this and next season and that there isn't anything but market manipulation to blame for the low price of oats.

Mon., Aug. 16. 37.

The terrible heat continues today. Our corn is standing it fairly well. There are spots in bad shape, but the main part of our fields would recover if rain would come in a day or too. That is, of course, if the wind and heat would let up.

I tried to plow stubble but the earth was too dry and hard.

Week of Aug. 18 to 24. 37.

Perhaps the most important happening of the week was the several showers of rain that fell. More rain than we have had in a like period for some time. It cooled and freshened the corn fields in nice shape. And it came without any wind or other ill effects. In our community it was not enough to complete the crop tho. It also was of much benefit to the parched pastures and moistened the fields for fall plowing.

Threshing is all completed in our run and all of the families gathered together one evening for a visit and ice cream was served by the machine operator.

The corn market continues to decline. Oats are at a standstill. I sealed my oats. The only farmer who has so far, in our neighborhood. I received 5 cents per bu. on them. The horse disease continues to invade new farm territory each week. Losses are heavy and can hardly be replaced.

Many farmers feel quite badly about the failure of the New Dealers to give agriculture the promised assistance. Farmers in general seem to be planning a way to get along some how. And I think many of them will, but it may not be so good for other folks a little later.

Sept. 1 to 4. 37.

Odd jobs and various things around the place these four days. The weather is quite warm and dry. Our corn fields are drying rather faster than they should. The drought is bad for the new seedings too.

We hear more and more about the disease, sleeping sickness, among the horses. New cases are developing rapidly. Many horses are dying. Stocks of vaccines and serums are rapidly becoming exhausted. Many and various remedies are being tried. And there are many ideas as to the cause of the sickness and how it is transferred from farm to farm.

Friday of this week I got medicine or vaccine from the drug store and gave it to our horses. It cost me 74 cents for the two horses I have.

Oct. 4. 37.

One of the most discussed topics among business men is "September Corn." The situation in the grain market during the later days of the month of September served to draw attention to the whole grain marketing system. I might say that, now, business men have worked two questions out of it. One of them, and the most frequently mentioned, is, why doesn't the government stop speculation and have this money come to the farmers, so they will have more to spend with business men. The other question is why doesn't the government see that speculation is taken out of the grain market and perhaps the farmers can make enough money that they will be able to get along without so much help from the government. This grain marketing subject has been much discussed at various times past. Sometime, possibly soon, something will be done about it.

Another thing that is coming close home to the people is the fight the telephone companies are making to stop, or delay the construction of the R.E.A. power and light lines. If it comes to the point where the farm folks must rebuild the telephone lines or do without the new power lines, they will do without the telephones. They say we will have cars anyway and phone service isn't dependable anyway.

Oct. 18. 37.

Farmers continue to discuss the R.E.A. and telephone line controversy. Many of them continue to say they would rather have the power and light than the phone, if they could have only one. And in this connection some farmers are saying that they think the Rural Free Delivery of mail might just as well be discontinued. What with cars, radios etc.

Nov. 9 to 14. 37.

The next few weeks will see the closing of field and crop work and in general the summing up of the season's accomplishments. Also Soil Conservation meetings will be held and interested committeemen are wondering how much interest will be shown.

Dec. 1. 37.

Fairly cold weather again today. The last time I sealed corn, Dec. 35 and sold it in 36, I or the secretary or the bank or someone failed to have it released. This must be done to clear the records for a new, present loan. I spent the day phoning and driving about this.

Prospects for an immediate loan are not promising. This is regretable. Whoever was to handle the loan has had since the farmers planted the corn crop to prepare for a loan. And it is a matter of common knowledge that many farmers were in the program mainly for the loan accommodation and some of them for no other reason.

Supplies and materials are not ready for use. Sealers have been instructed etc. But a delay must be endured. These things are what causes many farmers to remain out of government programs. This sealing idea did not suddenly come up and find things not prepared for it. It has been talked about and looked forward to thru the crop season.

Week of Dec. 11 to Dec. 17. 37.

The corn loan money came today, but it was too late to get it in the bank today. I received the full 50 cents per bu. I went to the office of the county treasurer and paid my taxes. He had very obligingly just let them wait. With the several tax reductions we were to have, I still paid as much as last year.

Rather bad weather today. I left the corn loan papers at the bank today, I signed my name 16 times on them.

Went to the bank today and renewed several notes. Paid one. Owe the bank $474 now. Attended a pancake and sausage supper this evening.

Dec. 25 to 31. 37.

As the year of 1937 is drawing to a close there are many things about the year that are better than last year were. The better grain crop being one of them. At least there has been much more feed for the livestock.

However, there have been unpleasant and regrettable things happen too. It seems to me that farm accidents have increased very greatly this past year. Especially tractor, ensilage cutter and corn picker accidents. It will take some time yet to educate farmers to exercise greater care in the use and operation of these machines.

From a business standpoint the very low price of the oats crop and the declining prices of hogs and cattle have been very discouraging to farmers. Then, too, the delay in making soil conservation payments is working a hardship on some farmers. The corn loan is thot by many to be of much help.

The badly muddled affairs of Congress and the Administration do not hold out too much promise for the coming year.

Two residents of Putnam County, Georgia.   *[Bureau of Agriculture Economics, National Archives.]*

CHAPTER SEVEN

Blacks in the New Deal Years

WALTER WHITE

Introduction by ROBERT L. ZANGRANDO

Being black in America always has held a special meaning: deprivation, humiliation, and oppression on the one hand; on the other, a racial and cultural consciousness derived from the Western Hemisphere and from Africa. For three and a half centuries, a mixture of force and choice, assigned status and self-identity has given Afro-Americans an unmatched sense of community.

That community found itself sorely tested between 1933 and 1945. The depression brought ruin to urban and rural blacks. World War II, despite extraordinary opportunities for national service, underscored, through discrimination and violence, the lack of rights and options possessed by black people.

Through the discrimination, hostility, and indifference in the North and West, and through the legalized segregation and Jim-Crowism of the South and border states, blacks (about 10 percent of the population) suffered disproportionately from unemployment and under-employment, residential crowding, disfranchisement, and a wide range of disabilities in public accommodations. In 1940, five percent of southern black adults were registered to vote. From 1929 to 1944, one of 435 congressional districts (located on Chicago's south side) elected a black man to the House of Representatives, and no black sat in the Senate. Until 1937, no black judge served on the federal bench. In 1939, only 99 of 774 public libraries in 13 southern states would serve black readers. In 10 southern states during 1935-1936, public school officials spent an average of $49.30 per white pupil and $17.04 per black student; that same year, those states allotted a mere three percent of public school transportation funds for black students, who comprised 28 percent of total enrollment. As late as the *Brown vs. Board of Education* decision of 1954, laws of 17 states and the District of Columbia required segregation.

In 1930, unemployment among black workers outside the South was just over 11 percent, contrasted with 7.4 percent for their white counterparts; 10 years later the comparison stood at 29 and 14.8 percent. In 1940, the median annual income for a black high school graduate was $775 compared to $1,454 for a white graduate; that of a black college graduate was only $1,074, contrasted with $2,046 for a white. Even wartime opportunities in military service or defense plants failed to correct the inequities. The armed forces maintained segregated units, while job discrimination in industry and in federal employment persisted throughout the war. By the autumn of 1946, unemployment rates for blacks were two to three times higher than for whites in 10 major cities throughout the East, Midwest, South, and border states.

Most debilitating of all was the violence inflicted by whites upon black Americans. This took the form of lynchings (whereby mobs assaulted and murdered defenceless victims), race riots (like that in Detroit during the summer of 1943), and random attacks on black soldiers stationed in the South during the war. Data collected by such agencies as the National Association for the Advancement of Colored People in New York City, Tuskegee Institute in Alabama, and the *Chicago Defender* newspaper indicated that from 1882 (the earliest year for reliable statistics) to 1960, lynch mobs killed over 4,730 persons; at least 3,341 of these were black people. The figures, of course, deal only with reported lynchings, and we have no way of knowing how many more went unrecorded. Moreover, there was the problem of "legal lynchings," whereby blacks were convicted of crimes they had not committed, as in the Scottsboro affair of the early 1930s.

For southern blacks, lynching was a particularly vicious phenomenon. Denied participation in the political and law enforcement processes, blacks remained acutely vulnerable whenever local white sentiment condoned mob violence. White lynchers almost always avoided punishment, although their identity was easy to determine. Often, local officials connived with lynch mobs. Despite assertions about "protecting" white womanhood, less than 30 percent of black lynch victims had ever been accused, let alone tried and convicted, of rape or attempted rape. From a high of 230 in 1892, lynching deaths declined to 28 in 1933, 15 in 1934, 20 in 1935, and thereafter never exceeded eight per year. Nonetheless, the phenomenon still displayed a highly racist character: of the 165 reported lynchings from 1930 through 1950, 151 involved black victims.

Working primarily through the NAACP, the black community and its supporters challenged these conditions. NAACP lawyers successfully attacked inequities in several areas, including education, voting rights, transportation, and housing. During the Roosevelt years they lost only one case in the United States Supreme Court. Civil rights forces also pressured the president. Educated by Eleanor Roosevelt to recognize the black community's needs and responsive to the growing importance of the black vote in northern cities, Franklin Roosevelt encouraged the appointment of a fairly sizeable number of black men and women to federal offices and advisory commissions. While most blacks in federal service held low paying jobs, their number did increase from about 50,000 in 1933, to 82,000 by 1938, and 200,000 by the end of 1946.

Nonetheless, many black activists felt that New Deal agencies either had not responded sufficiently or had not responded without discrimination to the needs of the black community during the depression. As a result, John P. Davis and others organized the all-black National Negro Congress in 1936 in a determined but largely ineffectual effort to improve matters. Undoubtedly the most dramatic and controversial federal action of the Roosevelt years came June 25, 1941, when the president by executive order created the Fair Employment Practice Committee (FEPC) to forestall a threatened march on Washington planned by A. Philip Randolph of the Brotherhood of Sleeping Car Porters and Maids. Randolph had demanded remedies for discrimination in three areas: factories that handled defense contracts, federal civil service employment, and the armed forces. The executive order ignored the military, and FEPC dealt mainly with injustices in defense-related industries. Although, even there the FEPC proved to be a paper tiger. The committee could investigate and recommend, but it lacked enforcement powers. Businessmen objected to inquiries into hiring and promotion practices. Conservative congressmen and senators of both major parties attacked the whole idea and terminated the committee in 1946.

While black leaders had limited success with the judicial and executive branches in the Roosevelt years, Congress persistently refused to enact civil rights measures. No such federal law had passed since 1875, and none would until the Civil Rights Acts of 1957, 1960, 1964, 1965, and 1968. In the New Deal years, southern Democrats, aided by conservative Republicans, regularly threatened filibusters to prevent such measures from coming to a Senate vote. Through seniority, these same southerners controlled most congressional committees, and Roosevelt declined to challenge them openly on behalf of civil rights proposals.

Meanwhile, the NAACP by the late 1930s had assembled a civil rights coalition to include the United Auto Workers, the National Urban League, the American Jewish Committee, the American Civil Liberties Union, the League for Industrial Democracy, the National Council of Churches, the Y.W.C.A., and several other reform and service organizations. The Communist Party of the United States and a southern liberal group known as the Commission on Interracial Cooperation (reorganized by 1944 as the Southern Regional Council) added outside momentum to the lobbying effort. Simultaneously, the C.I.C.'s Association of Southern Women for the Prevention of Lynching worked at state and local levels to combat racial mob violence.

The NAACP won House passage of a federal anti-lynching bill on three occasions (1922, 1937, and 1940), but the measure always died in the Senate. In the struggle to enlarge the voting rights of blacks and poor whites, the Southern Conference for Human Welfare (founded in 1938) and other civil rights advocates achieved House passage of the anti-poll tax bill five times (1942 to 1949). Not once did the bill reach the Senate floor. And, despite the efforts of Randolph's March on Washington Movement and of his National Council for a Permanent FEPC, Congress refused to create a statutory commission to combat job discrimination. One small indication of future developments emerged in 1942, however, with the founding of the Congress of Racial Equality, an organization dedicated to non-violent, participatory demonstrations. That approach would later prove decisive in producing the legislative triumphs of the late 1950s and the 1960s.

Assistant executive secretary of the NAACP from 1918 to 1930, and executive secretary until his fatal heart attack in 1955, Walter F. White personally investigated 41 lynchings and eight race riots. In 1929 he published his famous book, *Rope and Faggot: The Biography of Judge Lynch.* No one in America exceeded his knowledge of the subject or his intense determination to end mob violence. White and the NAACP advocated legislation for federal intervention whenever three or more persons lacking legal authority harmed or killed a victim, and the state, county, or municipality had taken no remedial action. They sought prosecution, fines, and imprisonment of delinquent law officers and financial penalties for the county or counties involved.

When he testified before a Senate Judiciary Subcommittee in February 1940[1] Walter White reenacted a scene that dated from 1918, when the association began its annual appeals for a federal antilynching law. During these hearings, Tom Connally (Democrat-Texas) renewed his assault on the NAACP's position and showed in his hostile questions why he had become the recognized leader of Senate anti-civil rights forces during the late 1930s and early 1940s. On the other side, New Deal Democrat Robert F. Wagner of New York displayed his commitment to the anti-lynching bill he had sponsored for the NAACP since 1934.

Consider these questions when examining the following document: What did it mean to be black in America in the 1930s? In what ways did the anti-lynching fight, focusing on the right to life, serve the civil rights movement as the opening wedge in the quest for federally sponsored interracial reform of the twentieth century? What are the strengths and limitations of a minority group's struggle for change through the political and legislative processes? In what ways might the anti-lynching fight have diverted attention and resources from other issues of crucial importance to the black community? Did America's sustained attention to international matters, before and during World War II, speed or retard the pace of interracial reform on the domestic front?

MR. WHITE: [The National Association for the Advancement of Colored People] is composed of individuals, whites and Negroes, northern and southern women, who felt something needed to be done to meet the rising tide of prejudice against Negroes in the United States. For 30 years we have been engaged in various fields, the field of legislation, of defense of Negroes charged with crime in an effort to see that they received a fair trial and were not convicted because of race prejudice.

We have done a good deal in the field of education. In these various fields we have had 13 cases in the United States

Supreme Court, and won 12 of them. In the thirteenth case the Court declared it was without jurisdiction. So our record has been fairly successful. . . .

The chief contention of opponents of this [anti-lynching] legislation in the House of Representatives, and one which undoubtedly will be made in the forthcoming debate in the Senate, is that lynchings in 1939 reached an all-time low of three according to the figures of Tuskegee Institute, or of five authenticated lynchings according to the National Association for the Advancement of Colored People.

It is therefore asserted that the lynching problem is solved and that there is no need of federal legislation.

Accepting for the moment that these three or five lynchings are all that took place during 1939, it is our contention that this in no way means that there is no need of an anti-lynching federal law. The history of this crime shows that the number of lynchings varies in an inverse ratio to the intensity of the campaign for federal legislation against lynching. When the campaign is vigorous, lynchings decrease; when the campaign is lessened, the curve of lynchings moves steadily upward. One of the South's most distinguished editors — Dr. Douglas S. Freeman, editor of the *Richmond* (Va.) *News Leader* and Pulitzer prize winner for his distinguished "Life of Robert E. Lee," writes me under date of January 27, 1940, apropos of this contention:

> I remain of opinion that the adoption of a suitable federal anti-lynching bill is essential to protect human life in the South, and to assure the results established in 1939. If the prospect of a federal anti-lynching law reduced lynching, the realities of such a law will prevent men permanently. Nothing else will. . . .

Other distinguished southern editors have written or told me within recent months that the chief factor in reducing lynching has been the threat of federal legislation. Many of them, who head influential newspapers in various parts of the South, have said to me that the agitation for a federal bill against lynching has been of inestimable help in that it has permitted them to say truthfully that if the South itself would not do something about lynching, passage of a federal law is inevitable. Remove this threat, many of these editors also assert, and lynching figures will mount.

It becomes increasingly evident, however, that the improvement is more apparent than real. The nationwide and worldwide publicity caused by lynching, and by the debate on the floor of Congress on the anti-lynching bill, has caused some reduction in lynching. But it is evident that there is as great need for federal aid to the states in suppressing lynching mobs as there ever was. In certain parts of the deep South mobs have adopted a new technique. Before the present nationwide interest in a federal anti-lynching bill, lynchings were staged frequently by mobs numbering as high as five and ten thousand men, women, and children. Sadistic torture of the helpless victim was frequently indulged in. Lynchings were advertised in advance through the press and over the radio. Fingers, toes, and other parts of the body were cut off and proudly retained as souvenirs. Impressionable children, their minds still plastic, were brought by their parents to view the horrible spectacle. But an aroused public conscience, including that of such powerful groups as the women of the Methodist-Episcopal Church, South, has made such orgies less popular. The mob now delegates the task of execution to a smaller group, usually consisting of 40 or 50 men, who take the victim into the woods or swamps, lynch him, dispose of his body, and thus keep the outside world from knowing what has happened.

Such a case was that of Joe Rodgers at Canton, Miss., last May 8. Rodgers was a hard-working, highly respected Negro citizen. He was a deacon in the local Baptist Church. His conduct was so exemplary that he had never had any difficulties with either the white or the colored people of Canton. He worked at a lumberyard. He was ordered by the foreman to move into a house owned by the company and to pay rent for it. Rodgers told the foreman that he already had a place to stay and preferred to remain there. When payday came on Saturday, Rodgers found that $4.50 had been deducted from his pay envelope for rental of the house he had not occupied. When he protested to the foreman and asked that this money be paid him, the foreman cursed him, struck him with his fist, and then seized a shovel and struck Rodgers. To protect himself from being seriously injured, Rodgers took the shovel away from the foreman. When the foreman rushed at him, Rodgers in self-defense hit the foreman with the shovel. To avoid further trouble, Rodgers went home.

He returned to work on Monday morning. He was seized by a mob, knocked unconscious, terribly beaten, and his skull fractured, and killed. His body was weighted with stones and thrown into the Pearl River.

It is probable that no one would ever have known of what had happened to Rodgers had not the stones become dislodged and Rodgers' body risen to the surface where it was seen by many white and Negro citizens of Canton. One of these citizens wrote to us. It is significant that this citizen, a highly respected, law-abiding individual, begged us not to reveal his name because, he declared, he would be treated as was Rodgers, were it to become known that he had revealed the lynching.

A distinguished southern white man was asked to investigate the case. He not only found the report of Rodgers' lynching to be true in every detail but also that there had been at least four other such lynchings in the vicinity of Cleveland, Miss., within a period of four months preceding the Rodgers lynching. It is significant that not one word of the Joe Rodgers or of these other four lynchings has ever been published in any newspaper as far as we are able to learn. God alone knows how many such lynchings have taken place in the rural areas of the South during the last few years about which the outside world knows nothing nor ever will know. . . .

The late James Weldon Johnson once declared in a public address that "lynching in the United States has resolved itself into a problem of saving black men's bodies and white men's souls. . . ." Lynching and the spirit of arrogant domination of those who indulge in it has done and is doing as much harm spiritually, mentally, and physically to those who dominate as it does to those whom lynching is designed to terrorize and intimidate. . . . The true significance of lynching is that it is primarily designed to intimidate not only Negroes but poor whites as well so as to keep them inferior in power and to prevent them from organizing or doing anything effective about low wages, hours of work, voting, obtaining justice in the courts, or otherwise improving their present miserable state.

It will be remembered that opponents of the anti-lynching bill, during the Senate debate of 1938, vigorously asserted that the states could and would stop lynching and punish lynchers if they were let alone. It will be remembered that Senator McKellar of Tennessee inserted into the Congressional Record telegrams from a number of southern governors making such assertions. But what are the facts? Since this bill was last before the Senate in 1938, there have been 11 thoroughly authenticated lynchings to say nothing of these additional cases which are just now coming to light. There has been not one conviction in any of these 11 cases and not even any arrests in 10 of the 11. . . . Not one of the 500 to 1,000 lynchers of 1939 was brought to trial and punished, or even arrested. Nor is there any real hope of such punishment of lynchers where Negroes are the victims as long as Negro citizens are disfranchised in certain states in open violation of the federal constitution. It is absurd to expect that a sheriff or other peace officer is going to risk defeat when he stands for reelection when the lynchers are the voters and the lynched are nonvoters. . . .

For more than two decades we have petitioned the Congress of the United States to pass a law to help the South and other parts of the country to free themselves from this menace of mob violence. Time and time again our plea has been denied by filibusterers who prevented the greatest deliberative body in the world from exercising its democratic right to vote up or down this type of legislation. That refusal to permit a vote is a denial of the democratic process, and it was done on the floor of the Senate.

In the meantime, democracy has been destroyed in other parts of the world, and is gravely threatened in our own beloved country. Who can tell how much of the spirit which has led to the formation of organizations like the Ku Klux Klan, the Black Legion, the bund, and the various "shirt" outfits, with their resort to direct action and a flouting of the law, is due to the disrespect for the law which lynchings over a period of a half century or more has created. Americans are alarmed, and rightfully so, at the growth of these subversive organizations which seek to destroy democratic governments. But if I were a Communist, a Nazi, or a Fascist and wanted to destroy or weaken American democracy, I would work unceasingly to prevent passage of anti-lynching legislation. If I wanted to convince 12 million American Negroes who constitute one-tenth of our population that they have no hope of justice under the American form of government, and wished to induce them to join a movement to overthrow democracy, I would oppose enactment of the anti-lynching bill because I could point to the continuation of lynching and all of the terrible things which the lynching spirit perpetuates as proof that they should no longer have faith in our form of government.

It is because we do believe that democracy, with all its shortcomings, is the best form of government yet devised that we urge the committee to report favorably and immediately upon this bill and to speed the bill to the floor of the Senate for temperate, intelligent debate and a vote. We urge those who truly love America to abstain from repetition of expensive filibustering which causes our government to be held up to ridicule here and abroad. All we ask is that members of the Senate, as representatives of the people of America, be permitted to vote, each of them, his or her conviction on this legislation. If the majority of the Senate should vote against the bill and defeat it, we, as good Americans, will accept that verdict without complaint. Is it too much to ask that opponents of this bill be willing to approach this subject in the same spirit?

The American people are overwhelmingly against our country's being involved in any war. But who can tell what will take place six months or a year hence? Members of the Senate are aware that public opinion may change if the forces of Hitler and Stalin and other totalitarian nations appear to be about to win. Despite the present state of public opinion in the United States, no sane and informed person can deny the possibilty that the United States may eventually be drawn into the second World War either to protect American lives or investments. Should that terrible eventuality become a reality, American Negroes will once again be called upon as Americans to bear their full share of the burden of war. They will be asked once again to die for democracy. I ask you, members of the Senate, to place yourselves in the position of the American Negro in the event of war. How would you feel about fighting for democracy for a country whose national legislative body refuses to pass a mild law against lynching? How would you feel if you put on the uniform of the United States Army, shouldered a rifle, bade your loved ones farewell, and went off to war with the realization that in your absence a lawless mob could take your father, mother, brother, or sister and lynch or burn them alive at the stake? If you say that such an idea is fantastic, I direct your attention to the lynching records of the years following the last World War when Negro soldiers, returned from France, were lynched because they wore the uniform of the country in whose defense they had fought in foreign lands.

We ask the United States Senate, for this and other reasons, that it pass the anti-lynching bill and not make it any more difficult to respect and love our native land. . . .

A few evenings ago, I talked with a small group of distinguished scientists in New York. Most of them were born in other countries and had emigrated to the United States, where they had contributed their great talents toward the enrichment of our national life and culture. One of them was a brilliant biochemist, who, though not a Jew, had fled from Nazi Germany because his conscience would not permit him to approve the Hitler regime which menaces the peace of the world. Another was a distinguished Swiss social scientist who is now an American citizen. A third was a famous writer. Someone asked, "What do you remember as the first thing you heard about America?" Promptly and unanimously each one of the three persons answered, "lynching!"

Should the Congress not pass this legislation and thereby show the world at large that the national government is against this terrible crime? The mere enactment of such a law would make more effective and less hypocritical and vulnerable our just condemnation of the oppression of racial and religious minorities in other countries. . . .

SENATOR CONNALLY: Do you believe in including all murders under this bill?

MR. WHITE: No, sir.

SENATOR CONNALLY: Do you believe in including gang murders in New York, as well as lynchings in the South?

MR. WHITE: Gang murders are not confined to New York.

SENATOR CONNALLY: I did not ask you that.

SENATOR WAGNER: Mr. Chairman, I think the witness should have the opportunity fully to answer the question before another question is asked.

SENATOR CONALLY: I listened to this man's full statement without interruption. I claim that I am entitled to inquire into the matters covered by his statement.

SENATOR WAGNER: I do not say that you are not.

SENATOR CONNALLY: I would like to have an answer to the question. . . .

MR. WHITE: It would seem to be sound legislative practice not to try to cover the whole world in one bill. This bill is aimed at a specific malady in American life — namely, lynching. It would seem to me the bill should be confined to the specific evil at which it is aimed. If someone wants to introduce another bill dealing with some other crime, that is perfectly agreeable, and would seem to me to be the proper procedure. . . .

SENATOR CONNALLY: Do you think that political motives influenced only those opposing the bill, or would you include a few on the other side?

MR. WHITE: Unquestionably some on the other side.

SENATOR CONNALLY: The opposition was more political than those who favored the bill?

MR. WHITE: That would amount to a discussion of metaphysics.

SENATOR CONNALLY: I know, but you are qualified to talk about metaphysics.

MR. WHITE: I do think that some of the opposition was political, although many of them admitted the Negro was disfranchised.

SENATOR CONNALLY: Do you mean to imply the Negroes are disfranchised in Texas?

MR. WHITE: Pretty largely so.

SENATOR CONNALLY: Have you ever been in Texas?

MR. WHITE: Yes, sir. They almost lynched me in Dallas last year.

SENATOR CONNALLY: Almost?

MR. WHITE: Yes. . . .

SENATOR CONNALLY: More than three formed a mob and took after you?

MR. WHITE: Would you be interested in hearing the story?

SENATOR CONNALLY: I want to know if more than three persons were after you.

MR. WHITE: Quite a group.

SENATOR CONNALLY: Did they catch you?

MR. WHITE: They did not have to. I stayed right there.

SENATOR CONNALLY: Were you molested in any way?

MR. WHITE: I was threatened. . . .

SENATOR CONNALLY: And you were not harmed? You might have been frightened, but you were not harmed, were you?

MR. WHITE: I was not particularly frightened. I was protected by Texas people, both black and white. I was passing through from Oklahoma to Galveston, and had to lay over five hours in Dallas. When I arrived, I found a considerable crowd there, apparently taking some interest in me. They had arranged a meeting for me at the Y.W.C.A. . . . It seems there had been a protest made to the mayor against the meeting. . . . The sheriff and the mayor told them they could not prevent the meeting.

SENATOR CONNALLY: Do you mean to say that the officers protected and defended you?

MR. WHITE: They told them there was no legal way of stopping it. Threats were made about what would happen if the meeting was held. When I reached the city, the local people who had arranged the meeting told me about it. . . . They told me they had to move the meeting . . . because the people who had charge . . . feared there might be trouble. The meeting was held in the colored Y.M.C.A. building.

SENATOR CONNALLY: And you spoke?

MR. WHITE: I did speak.

SENATOR CONNALLY: You were not molested?

MR. WHITE: No. There were some threats made.

SENATOR CONNALLY: They did not bother you?

MR. WHITE: I don't think it would have been wise to do that.

SENATOR CONNALLY: I asked you if you were bothered.

MR. WHITE: No.

SENATOR CONNALLY: I thought not. That is all. . . .

SENATOR WILEY: [R.-Wis.] I would like to have you state on the record what argument whites in the South have against this. Why are they fearful of this proposed law?

MR. WHITE: It is my impression, and I have traveled a good deal in the South and am acquainted with a good many, both white and colored, that the people in the South are not against it. The Gallup poll shows 64 percent favoring a federal law against lynching. . . .

SENATOR WILEY: What are the objections of those who are against it?

MR. WHITE: The chief argument seems to be that it is an invasion of states' rights.

SENATOR WILEY: I am a novice in the Senate. I wonder if you know of other arguments, and how you would apply them.

MR. WHITE: There has been so much said on the floor of Congress that has no relation to the bill —

SENATOR WILEY: Never mind that.

MR. WHITE: Yet there has been a great mass of material used in filibustering back and forth since 1922. I would say the principal argument is on the question of invasion of states' rights. There is also the argument that the South knows how to handle its own problem better than the federal government knows how to handle it. I think that is about all that can be classified.

SENATOR WAGNER: Speaking of the invasion of states' rights, if a man is charged with an offense, and the record shows that he has not been given a fair and impartial trial according to due process, and he was not accorded the equal protection of the law, under the federal Constitution the United States Supreme Court takes jurisdiction.

MR. WHITE: Yes, eventually.

SENATOR WAGNER: Without any specific legislation, based upon the Fourteenth Amendment to the Constitution.

MR. WHITE: That is correct.

SENATOR WAGNER: Take the Scottsboro case. That case came up from Alabama to the United States Supreme Court, on the ground that is was a violation of the Fourteenth Amendment to the Constitution. The Court took jurisdiction, and found that the defendant had not been accorded equal protection of the law.

There was a record upon which the Court could act. Now here, as I understand the history of lynching, no such protection was ever accorded to the man who was lynched. He is never brought into court. If he were brought into court and tried, then the United States Supreme Court could determine whether or not the Fourteenth Amendment had been violated. The difficulty is that through the neglect of someone, the man really charged with the commission of a crime cannot be produced in court. He is taken and lynched without a trial. In one case we have the protection of the trial in court, to determine whether the individual received the protection to which he was entitled under the Fourteenth Amendment. In the other case there is no such opportunity.

So, as I understand Senator Wiley's suggestion, there might be some difficulty in determining the jurisdiction of the state or federal court. In the one case, if a man's rights are violated, he has a right to go to the United States Supreme Court and have that question determined. Our complaint is that in these lynching cases there has been no trial. In many instances there has been no effort made to apprehend those who are charged.

MR. WHITE: That is correct.

SENATOR WAGNER: Under this act, if such a lynching occurs, if the officer has been criminally negligent in failing to prevent a lynching, then he is guilty of a crime.

Notes

1.   U.S. Senate, Committee on the Judiciary, *Crime of Lynching: Hearings before a Subcommittee* (76th Cong., 3rd Session; Washington, 1940), 51-74.

The old and new South, Ensley, Alabama. [Farm Security Administration photo, Library of Congress Prints and Photographs Division]

CHAPTER EIGHT

World War II: The Southern Experience

Introduction by DAVID H. CULBERT

When the Japanese attacked Pearl Harbor on December 7, 1941, America finally found herself at war with Japan, and, within a few days, Germany and Italy. The total war which followed affected communities, family life, and the average American, whether soldier or civilian. The impact of war is not just to be found in accounts of how President Franklin D. Roosevelt, British Prime Minister Winston Churchill and Soviet Premier Josef Stalin plotted the course of war at the highest level. What follows is not the tale of generals and presidents but the experience of real persons — residents of the South — who were vitally influenced by what happened between 1940 and 1945.

The date 1940 is significant. By no means did the United States spring from a nation at peace to a nation at war on December 7, 1941. By September 1940 with the Destroyer-Bases Agreement, the United States not only promised 50 overage destroyers to Britain but spiritually linked this country to the fate of Britain's battle against Hitler. War was not inevitable in 1940, but millions of Americans realized that a decade of economic depression was coming to an end. The average American took a little extra money home; jobs became more plentiful because of such things as "war work" or "defense contracts." America, although technically at peace, began to increase supplies needed for war. In the words of Franklin Roosevelt, America in 1940 became the "Great Arsenal of Democracy." In March, 1941, Congress passed the Lend-Lease Act, which permitted the sending of vast amounts of war material to countries fighting Adolf Hitler's Germany and Benito Mussolini's Italy. With so much earlier activity, it would be unwise to think of America's involvement in World War II as beginning only after the attack on Pearl Harbor.

World War II produced a social revolution in American society, both for the millions of men in the armed forces, and for the civilian population. Millions of Americans moved to distant parts of the country seeking new jobs. Military bases and defense industries altered many communities. The result was unintended reform and a society strikingly similar to that of today — both the good and bad. The South experienced these changes in a particularly dramatic fashion. It had long been the least industrialized, least prosperous section of the country. The war brought factories, army camps, and northerners by the thousands into the South, and at the same time permitted many natives to glimpse firsthand life outside the region. As a result, the South rapidly drew much closer to being in step with the rest of the nation. Modern American society may owe more to economic, social, and technological change in the early 1940s than to all the speeches and promises of the 1930s.

Obviously, a few readings cannot describe the entire war or its total impact on a population of more than 130 million. The following selections, however, vividly describe some of the effects World War II had on the United States and on the South in particular. All are based on family history projects written by students at Louisiana State University between 1972 and 1975 and deposited in the LSU Library, Department of Archives and Manuscripts. Students conducted recorded interviews with their parents and grandparents. The words are those of the students, except that last names have been changed and occasional misspellings of certain cities and towns have been silently corrected.

The individual and family experiences raise interesting questions about the war. Are the experiences of these people representative of what happened to Americans during World War II? Can a government in wartime afford to carefully preserve the rights of every individual? What sorts of persons represent "a clear and present danger" to national security? How did the war affect family and community life, dating and marriage? Did military life help persons find fulfillment and prepare them for postwar life?

CIVIL LIBERTIES — During World War I, President Woodrow Wilson, in order to wage the "war to end all wars" more effectively, silenced opposition at home. The result was wholesale abridgment of civil liberties and such notorious laws as the Sedition Act of 1918 which made it a crime punishable by imprisonment to criticize any aspect of the war effort. In World War II Franklin D. Roosevelt was determined to avoid Wilson's extremism if possible. Most historians agree that America entertained dissent more successfully during World War II, with the exception of the rounding up of more than 100,000 Japanese-Americans, mostly on the West coast, in 1942. These Nisei were isolated in armed camps. No attempt was made to round up only acknowledged spies or to discover what the attitudes of individual Japanese-Americans were towards the war. Many since 1945 have judged Roosevelt harshly for these steps, pointing to the impact of such American-style concentration camps on tiny children and the aged, calling the action morally indefensible, and denying that such an extreme policy could be defended in terms of wartime necessity.

Many Americans never knew about the Japanese-American roundup at the time, but today the history of wartime civil liberties threatens to become the record of only the Nisei. What about German-Americans and Italo-Americans? The former, in World War I, had been subjected to all sorts of harassment, often because of "crimes" such as having a German family name. The following incidents took place in Louisiana between 1940 and 1945. The first concerns Italo-Americans; the second, a German-American family.

An Italo-American During the War

During World War II, Luciano [who had operated a grocery store in Bossier City, Louisiana, since 1912] was classified an enemy alien. He had made his declaration of intention to become a citizen on August 17, 1909, but had never applied for citizenship. The sheriff of Bossier Parish came and took away all of his radios and guns and knives. Since Luciano knew the sheriff, he was allowed to keep one butcher knife for use in the store. Everything was returned at the end of the war.

Recollections of a German-American Family

Father was born in Dresden, Germany, in 1897. He bummed a ride over on a trans-[Atlantic] steamer of some sort. Entered the U.S.A. illegally in about 1910. In 1914 he and my mother got married. My mother was 15 at the time. She was from Mississippi, and he was still a very avid German, a "they-were-going-to-rule-the-world"-type person.

They lived in Bogalusa [Louisiana] but right after they got married they moved to Baton Rouge. They rented this real old beat-up house. The rent at this time was $100 a year and there was 12 acres of land with it. My father was a farmer, and he was a carpenter. His primary crop was tomatoes.

Very pro-German [in 1917-18]. Made a lot of bad maneuvers. They owned a Model T Ford. Some Germans who had escaped from a prison [er-of-war] camp somewhere had my father's name and address as one of their contacts. Well, a group of them came to the house one night and he gave them the car, some food, all the money he had and they left. About two days later the authorities brought the car back. They had caught the prisoners and the prisoners swore they stole it [the car] and my father said yes they must have stole it.

In about 1941 my oldest brother joined the navy. My father is still preaching "Heil Hitler," "long live Germany," and this sort of bit. He was a very domineering person, and my mother practically would never question him. Besides you have to remember that we had eight children [in the family].

We did not have electricity. No, we did not have running water. Tomatoes were our number one product but we had all sorts of vegetables and one of our big selling points was at the farm; people used to drive out from the city [2 miles] to pick up the vegetables. I can remember the discussions. You know, "Oh, get the hell out of here;" "Germany's gonna win this war." Sometimes it was just a matter of discussion with people he knew. But often times he was doing it with people he didn't know.

They definitely knew he was German. Around town, while we were getting our hair cut he would go next door and have a beer and eat hot tamales and you could hear in between the walls hollering about who was going to win the war.

It would have had to have been about the year '42. Again

we [America] established a German prisoner-of-war camp around Lake Charles [Louisiana]. Our name was on the F.B.I.'s list of those people who would be sympathetic to the Germans, and we immediately had a visit from the F.B.I. I remember they took our radio. We had a big console battery-operated radio because we didn't have electricity. And the batteries in the back were not what we think of [as] batteries. These were the big cell batteries like you put in your car. Real good battery. No trouble picking up [shortwave broadcasts from Germany]. My mother really got torn up about the radio, and she went downtown and for her that was quite a chore because she usually had to bum a ride. She didn't even have a driver's license. She wasn't allowed to drive the car [by my father] even though she knew how. She raised all kinds of hell about it, and they brought the radio back. But they kept the battery. So we didn't have a radio anyway. Didn't have any money so that solved that problem. They [also] took our .410 shotgun and they took our .22 rifle. Of course our only form of entertainment was the radio. Especially at night or whatever because we lived so far from town we only got in town to see a movie once a month or something. The shotgun and the rifle were aggravating because that was one of our sources of food. We hunted many times.

My father was very tight. Spending money wasn't one of his virtues. He had the money, he had the car, see, where no one else could.

It wasn't very long [before] the paper boy would no longer deliver the paper. He was very straightforward. He was told that we were no longer to get a paper. That it was a means of communication and that was not allowed. About this time family relations between mother and father became very strained, if that is the right word for it. So he didn't stay at home very often. But that didn't change anything in the house. The postmaster decided that he would no longer deliver the mail to our house, says, "well if you want your mail you can go to Twin Cedars [two miles away]." Didn't get a whole lot of mail anyway. All we got was letters from friends and all. We didn't get any mail; we no more had a newspaper. We didn't have a radio; we didn't have any guns. [For a] relatively short period of time some law enforcement agency, when notified of a prison escape [prisoner-of-war camp], would come out and take our automobile.

The car was never totally taken away. It was only taken away whenever there apparently was a prison break. Remember when we go back to World War I there was records to the fact that he gave the car. The law enforcement agencies would come and say — they knew my mother by name — "Myrtle, got some escaped prisoners. Gonna be taking your car again." More often than not when someone came to the door my father would go out the back door and you wouldn't see him anymore.

This was my father's car. Which, of course, remember only he drove. They never took his truck because it was his only means of income. In fact, my number two brother was exempt from the service because he lived on a farm.

[These disabilities] really didn't change our way of life. Because our way of life, in my case, was to get up, milk the cows and do whatever, walk to school usually, come home from school and work the farm. The only person who wrote us a little that seemed important to my mother was my brother who was in the service [in the Pacific]. So this continued for some period of time. I have a feeling that this all came to a total halt when my father left home [for good]. This must have been very early in '44.

WARTIME COMMUNITIES — Training a huge army necessitated the establishment of large army camps throughout the United States. Each camp introduced trainees to an unfamiliar part of the country (Many a northerner never forgot basic training in such places as Louisiana and Mississippi in August). But just as important, the camp transformed communities and families in the surrounding areas. This excerpt describes what happened to a poor Louisiana family and a rural community when the opening of a nearby army camp created wartime prosperity. Notice that economic gain did not necessarily lead to universal improvement.

As sawmills closed because of both the economic depression and decreasing timber supplies, unemployment levels rose. A government-sponsored program, the Civilian Conservation Corps, paid a dollar for a 10-hour work day, and Isaiah [Bryan] was hired to plant pine seedlings in the Woodworth area south of Alexandria. (He walked 15 miles to and from work during this period except for the brief time he rented a small house near the CCC headquarters.)

During the 30s, in the small community of McNary, neighbors met weekly for prayer meetings, and on Saturday nights had community plays and "singings." They played dominoes, or "rooks," made divinity candy, and listened to Victrola records from mail-order catalog stores. Alice [Bryan] and a friend sometimes worked crossword puzzles while the men talked [Huey] "Long" politics.

Cooperation was the way of life; Alice did laundry for a neighbor while the neighbor sewed for both families. The men of the community shared such items as "tooth pullers" and shoe lasts, and garden implements and produce. One man even risked his life extingushing a fire caused by a faulty flue in the wood heater that warmed the small house rented by the Bryans.

The 1940s saw numerous changes in the area, mainly economic. The sprawling complex known as Camp Claiborne (the army training camp located seven miles north of McNary) brought job opportunities, transportation with its fleet of buses traveling to Oakdale and to Alexandria, and entertainment at its theaters and coliseum.

Families invited soldiers to their homes for Sunday dinner and were exposed to customs and ideas alien to their sheltered lives.

Isaiah first worked at the army camp as a carpenter with his pay starting at $.76 an hour and advancing to $.84 an hour. As a guard, he earned $1,770, then $2,093 per annum.

Family income increased, too, from the rent paid by a soldier and his wife for the one room which they rented from the Bryans. Alice worked as a clerk in the community grocery store, and the oldest daughter worked as a typist at Camp Claiborne.

McNary was a place of convenience during these times. In Glenmora, one mile south, were churches, drug stores, garages, hardware stores, a "five-and-dime" store, a post office and the school. A small medical clinic, two doctors, and a dentist served the community. Alexandria, 25 miles north, and Oakdale, 12 miles south, met additional needs.

In this small community with approximately three dozen

houses and one grocery store, staples and fresh bread could be purchased, though a loaf of bread now [c. 1942] cost 10 cents rather than a nickel. Daily newspapers were brought by bus and purchased by the residents, and mail was delivered on weekdays by a rural route driver. An iceman from the plant in Glenmora delivered large 10-cent blocks of ice to the customers' boxes, and a Rapides Parish Book Mobile made weekly visits to the area.

Community customs changed rapidly: as radios became common, and the number of automobiles increased mobility, community "get-togethers" became rare. As the "outer world" was brought into the area, young people were not permitted to walk to Glenmora at night. The many hoboes that had previously been given food at back doors were now unwelcome.

Isaiah continued to work at Camp Claiborne, a short three-mile journey through the pine woods. He also improved the house, including wiring for the electricity that had at last reached this area. No longer were kerosene lamps filled and chimneys cleaned; black smoothing irons became book ends, the radio no longer faded out because of dead batteries, and best of all, deep wells run by electricity permitted indoor plumbing.

In McNary, where most of her childhood was spent, Sybil [Isaiah and Alice's daughter] and friends played on the concrete foundations which remained near the mill ponds of earlier sawmilling days. While their parents planted "victory gardens," they played war games, forming "Junior Commandoes." At the community store they listened to the talk of the maneuvering soldiers from Camp Caliborne. They were given shoulder chevrons and insignias, received "V"-mail, and were taught such songs as "Remember Pearl Harbor."

During these early 40s which spanned Sybil's pre-teen and early teen years, the rapidly-changing economy permitted money for entertainment. Groups walked the mile from McNary to Glenmora to view the movie hits of such stars as Betty Grable, Clark Gable, Bob Hope, and Bing Crosby. They also enjoyed "shoot-em-ups," "Our Gang" comedies, and the Captain Marvel stories.

The battery-operated radio was another source of entertainment, with favorite programs being Red Skelton, Bob Hope, "Fibber McGee and Molly," and "Amos and Andy."

Sybil and her friends wore jeans or full ballerina skirts, frilly "Gibson-girl" blouses, and saddle-oxford shoes. They read *Miss America* magazine, used the current expressions such as "Hubba! Hubba!" and learned to "jitter-bug" to the records of the big bands.

DATING AND MARRIAGE — Wartime was time for romance. Soldiers were sent all over the United States before being sent overseas. Wherever they went, they met new girls, or were followed by old girlfriends, wives and families. Wartime did not mean that everyone planted a "victory garden" or thought only about how to beat the Germans and the Japanese. For many it was a time to find a husband or have fun. The following excerpts describe a 16 year-old girl's reaction to wartime New Orleans and the experiences of a college girl from West Virginia who met her future husband while a student at the University of Alabama. Be sure to notice not just problems of dating and marriage, but details of college life in wartime, as well as social activity in a large city.

A Teenager in World War II

In 1944, Marilyn's [a 16 year-old New Orleans girl] social life very quickly got into full swing. Greek life meant sock hops, winter and summer formals, gatherings in the French Quarter, nightclubs, and movie theaters. On Saturdays, Beta Delta [sorority] would host luncheons, sometimes in the Blue Room of the Roosevelt [Hotel] where such "greats" would play as Frankie Laine and his Orchestra and others. As for the music which dominated the social scene of the young New Orleanian . . . Frank Sinatra was of course the first of the bobby sox idols. Harry James and his Orchestra, too, were very highly revered.

And then there was World War II. "Everybody was so patriotic." A port city, New Orleans was a naval base and charged with the wartime atmosphere. The songs, the movies, the books, all reeked of a "soldier boy" scent. Between movies at the theaters, news reels were unleashed presenting the actual fighting. Marilyn's brother Jimmie tried to join up but was turned down because of poor eyes.

Upon Mary Kate's wall at home was a gigantic world map with little flags in each geographical location of a fighting nephew, son, or close friend. Her home was one of many that proudly displayed a symbol in the window indicating a member of the family was at war.

As for Marilyn, she remembers the excitement more than the horror. Just at the dating age, it seemed that every weekend she and her father were driving down to the train station to see a soldier off, or to greet him coming in. As many of the boys she dated joined the fighting, she soon began receiving letters from all over the world. She missed the boys, yes, yet it was exciting for her, too. Somehow, men in uniform, always seemed to irradiate a special appeal.

Account of a Wartime Romance

Teenagers in high school [in Matoaka, West Virginia] were aware of the world situation, but none of them suspected the day of doom that would thrust our nation into a world war before the year was over, so they were a pretty carefree bunch. It was during a Sunday drive with a boyfriend that my mother heard the dreadful news over the car radio — the Japanese had attacked Pearl Harbor. The next thing they knew, President Roosevelt had declared the country in a state of war. For the next few weeks, news broadcasts were sent to the classrooms over the P.A. system. In Matoaka everyone went to the high school auditorium to pick up ration books. Within the next few months, all physically fit young men were drafted or enlisted and many people in town left for the cities to work in defense plants. During those months, old and young alike jumped on the band wagon for the good of the country. In the course of those months, there was little to look forward to except graduation. Finally graduation exercises came and went. With some guidance from her father, my mother decided to go the University of Alabama in the fall. The rest of the summer was dull because there were no jobs for girls of that age in Matoaka, so she helped around the house and made plans for the fall.

One Sunday evening in 1942, my mother boarded the bus for Tuscaloosa [Alabama]. In the 40s there was no commercial airport or direct train route to the south. Buses were not air-conditioned and had no restrooms on board. She rode all night and all the next day, changing buses in Knoxville, Chatanooga, and Birmingham. Late Monday she arrived in Tuscaloosa.

In late February of the following year [1943], Betty, a girlfriend from home, came to the university to enroll. Along with Betty's arrival came hordes of men in uniform to the campus [for military training] and filled the men's dorms that were vacant. Through Betty's arrangement of a blind date for my mother with a serviceman, my parents met and fell in love.

My mother followed my dad's progress through his letters and he went to see her on his first leave. My dad [now in Europe] was closer to combat duty than before and the future was still uncertain. After he had been gone a few days, he sent her his fraternity pin. It was accepted as a bond between them in hopes that they would have time together another day. In the weeks that followed, she received letters from my dad from Brazil, the coast of Africa, and his destination in Italy, where the crew was based with the Fifteenth Air Force. In July of 1944, the letters from my dad stopped coming. She waited several weeks and finally there was a letter from him. On a mission to the Ploesti oil fields in Rumania, their plane had been hit and was disabled. Though badly wounded my dad said he was getting good care. Dad came back by boat and arrived at Portsmouth [Virginia] harbor in late October and it was on this leave in November of 1944 that he proposed to my mother and they became engaged.

IN THE SERVICE OF YOUR COUNTRY — During World War II, millions of Americans served in the army, navy, Marine Corps, and Army Air Corps (as the air force was then known) to say nothing of special branches for women. But soldiers are usually thought of as soldiers and not as individuals who come from families and communities where they have some sense of group identity. Also, most soldiers never saw actual combat. The following excerpts suggest two facets of wartime experience. The first is about a war hero, a man decorated for bravery and a flier who seems to have genuinely loved his military experience. Indeed after the war he found it difficult to return to civilian life and sought, in vain, some job which would permit him to continue the excitement of flying and, perhaps, the thrill of combat. The second excerpt consists of selections from letters written by a young sailor in 1945-46. He was stationed in the Pacific but the formal surrender of Japan in August 1945 found him still in basic training. He saw no action and was not decorated for bravery. The thrill of military life was lost on him.

A Dedicated Soldier

My father wanted to join the infantry. Unfortunately, his GCT [intelligence] score was so high that he was placed in the Army Air Corps. He was then sent to Keesler Air Force Base in Biloxi, Mississippi. When he arrived there, it was a tent-camp with 5,000 men. Nine months later, it was a fully staffed training camp with 85,000 men.

My father continued to do well on his aptitude tests. He broke the record scores on his induction tests. From Keesler Field he was sent to Lowrey Field in Denver, Colorado, for bombsight school, then to Arlington, Texas, for air gunnery school. He was assigned to the 525th Squadron (each squadron consisted of 12 planes) of the 379th Heavy Bombardment Group, in Boise, Idaho. The group formed in Salt Lake City, Utah, where they received their airplanes. These planes were the Boeing B-17 bombers, the Flying Fortresses. His first mission was at Hammer Field in Fresno, California, where his group carried out anti-submarine patrol with depth charges. There apparently was some fear about submarine shelling of the Pacific coast by the Japanese. Fortunately, these fears were groundless, particularly in light of the fact that my father's plane flew six missions before they learned that they were supposed to fuse the depth charges. An armorer asked them, quite by accident, when they fused the charges; the entire crew gave him a blank look and asked, "What fuse?" Somehow my father still received a special commendation for flying so many missions.

He, along with his squadron, was then sent to Mitchell, South Dakota, for additional bombing and gunnery range training. By this time my father was a sergeant. Unfortunately, one day as he was in the side gunner position shooting at a marked cliff, he got a bit over-enthusiastic and shot some of the tail off his own plane. He was soon a private again. From Mitchell he went to Sioux City, Iowa, for transitional and long-range bombing training. Then he was sent to Beth Page, New York, the site of the Grumman factory, where modifications were made on his plane. It is interesting to note that, once assigned to a particular plane and crew, you stayed with that same crew.

His squadron then flew the Atlantic by way of Goose Bay, Labrador; Rekjavik, Iceland; and Scotland. His group was assigned to an RAF airbase in Kimbolton, Bedfordshire [England]. My father was temporarily reassigned to an RAF base in cadre in Blackpool to teach the RAF people how to run the B-17, since they were getting a number of them on lend-lease. Bombing, by night, which had been the basic British philosophy of bombing, precluded the use of B-17s by the British, except for submarine patrol. The Army Air Corps, rather than using saturation bombing at night, developed completely accurate bombing by day.

My father was then sent back to Kimbolton for regular duty with his squadron. He participated in the first American air-raids over "Festung Europa;" his first raid was over the submarine pens in St. Lazaire. The RAF had been bombing them for months, with no result. My father's armor group obtained some British 16-inch armor-piercing shells, and imaginatively fashioned berths for them in the B-17. These shells destroyed the pens.

During this time, my father received the Bronze Star for redesigning the Norden bombsight for use in the European theater. The B-17s would fly together for massed firepower, and had no fighter escort. Therefore the utmost precision was needed. My father modified the sight so that the lead plane could drop on signal, and the compensation was automatically adjusted for the other planes in the group. He also received the Distinguished Flying Cross with one oak leaf cluster, and the Air Medal, with five oak leaf clusters.

Of all these statistics, the one which made the greatest impression on me was the following: out of 120 men originally with him in his squadron, only three survived the war without casualty or being taken as a P.O.W. I also found his descriptions of the escape routes out of France fascinating. He described the survival kit each man carried with him: dextrose tablets, high energy chocolate, benzedrine tablets, local maps (printed on silk), and, most interesting of all, counterfeit French or German money. I imagine this served the dual purpose of providing cash for the airman, and weakening the currency of the area.

In all, my father flew 56 missions. He was on the lead team, principally because he was qualified to do everything but pilot: he was an air mechanic, engine mechanic, electronics specialist, bombsight specialist, gunner, and wireless operator. He still has most of the strike photos from his missions. He was one of a group of men who had developed, during the war, a love of aviation.

Letters from a Sailor

Camp Lawrence, July 19, 1945

Dear Folks,

You know I only have just about four more weeks before I'll be home, and those coons and fish had better watch out — Don and I have been talking over what we were going to do when we get home.

Last Friday we went to the rifle range and I made the highest score in the company, which was 140 out of a possible 150 — we were shooting 30 cal. rifles. It was my first time to shoot them too. We shot at 200 yards.

That just goes to show you what farm life and hunting can do for one. It's a lot of city boys in the company, and we have arguments on the farm and city life — us farm boys come out on top every time too — they'll never convince me that there's a better life than the outdoor life and a life on the farm where there's the best family in the world.

You know, after the war when everything gets started again, I'd like to put up a sporting goods store around Cheneyville [Louisiana] — people really need one too. Don't give this idea away cause somebody might beat me to it. (ha) I guess I'd have to let daddy run it cause he would be my biggest customer . . .

Camp Lawrence, August 14, 1945,
[formal surrender of Japan; end of World War II]

I guess you all have heard the good news — I'm so thankful — I know everybody is — maybe it won't be too long before all of us can be home again and do all the things we planned. I guess we'll have quite a dog kennel now that there's six more hounds around. Don't give any away until I get there now.

Camp Aiea, Hawaii, September 26, 1945

We were hauling some garbage out to a big dump the other day — you should see the stuff they waste — no wonder there's a shortage at home — they throw away all kinds of radio equipment, furniture of all kind, and just lots of other things . . .

On board *Ernestine Karanda*, October 20, 1945

We have been going since the 4th — supposed to be in Manila tomorrow morning where we will get off. I don't know where we'll go then — This is a hospital ship we're on.

We passed a shot-up life-raft yesterday — had a shirt or something hanging on a stick — nobody was in it tho. No telling who was in it or what happened to them.

Manila, The Philippines, November 3, 1945

I went on liberty in Manila a couple of times — it's torn up a good bit and it's just filthy — I don't see how the people live. Beggars and people all over the place trying to sell anything they can. Prices are really high too — a shoe shine is $.50, cold drinks $.50, about three bananas for $.50 . . . everything is that way.

Yokahama, Japan, January 20, 1946

I finally started to write again — when I first got on this ship I thought I would be writing all the time, but now I know it's different. It's just so hard to write — I can't very well explain it but time just doesn't have any value at all. . . . We've been here in Japan since Nov. 19 — just transferring men and equipment from one place to another. We first came up here to Yokahama. . . . Tokyo, Yokahama, are really torn up, a lot of it is just level, can't tell if there ever was anything standing. . . . I don't see how Japan lasted as long as she did — there's hardly anything to this place — everytime I go on liberty I see· thousands of people and I haven't figured out yet where all of them stay.

Yokahama, Japan, February 24, 1946

I'm afraid to tell you how much I weigh — you might think I'm eating too much. Well, if you must know, I weigh just 220. I can just hear Daddy now, saying, "Just wait till he gets home, I'll work some of that off him."

I don't know if I'll ever get married — I just want to come back to the farm and live a life that I was meant to live.

Ironically, home was not the same after being in the service. This sailor ended up marrying a Spaniard and has lived all over the world thanks to his job as a petroleum engineer. Perhaps the navy experience did more for him than he recognized at the time.

Franklin Roosevelt addressing a nation-wide radio audience in 1942. [Office of War Information, National Archives.]

CHAPTER NINE

Rationing, Scrap Drives, and the Rubber Crisis

FRANKLIN ROOSEVELT AND FULTON LEWIS, JR.

Introduction by DAVID H. CULBERT

Managing the most complex war in history posed enormous problems for the United States. A huge war machine had to be created, millions of workers allocated between industry and the military, vital resources conserved, and the entire effort financed without completely upsetting the nation's economy. Drawing on the experience of the New Deal years, the federal government accepted these enlarged responsibilities. Many new agencies were created, and the federal civilian work force expanded from one million in 1940 to 3.8 million by 1945. The growth of government bureaucracy to administer the war effort became one of the most striking features of World War II, ushering in an era of increased government involvement in American life. The rubber crisis provides an especially vivid and significant example of the problems in government regulation of private industry.

The fall of Singapore to the Japanese on February 6, 1942, more than the attack on Pearl Harbor, drove home the reality of war. The much-discussed matter of "strategic materials" necessary for the war suddenly was defined in terms of one item: rubber. At one stroke, America lost the source of 90 percent of its annual natural rubber supply. The war, at first so distant and perhaps a bit unreal, now concerned millions of Americans in their daily lives. Some seriously proposed putting the nation on bicycles for the duration of the war. The resulting confusion resembled the energy crisis of recent years.

Throughout the spring and summer of 1942, all sorts of self-appointed spokesmen offered solutions to the rubber crisis. Basically there were two ways to deal with the problem:

drastically reduce civilian use of rubber; or find a substitute — either natural rubber from another part of the world or a synthetic rubber.

The first approach led to rationing of gasoline to cut down on civilian driving and reduce tire wear. Gasoline became the first of many items which civilians had difficulty getting in quantity during the war. The Office of Price Administration (OPA), amidst continuing confusion, issued to families throughout the entire country coupons which allowed them to purchase limited amounts of gasoline, sugar, meat, and a variety of other foodstuffs and raw materials needed for the military. Also, prices were fixed by the OPA. Thus, government rationing, not supply-and-demand, regulated the consumer market. Civilian production of new automobiles was banned for the war's duration. Many other goods, such as silk stockings, became virtually impossible to obtain. Such restrictions proved frustrating to the many bestowed with money from wartime prosperity. Most citizens patriotically supported the OPA, but some — to this day nobody can say how many — used the black market.

The second method for combatting the rubber shortage led to a search for substitute rubber. A trickle of natural rubber entered the United States from Brazil and Liberia. Not much more helpful was a heralded scheme where citizens patriotically collected scrap rubber from old automobile tires, door mats, and rubber hoses. There existed a limited amount of scrap rubber. Rumors of hoarding made the rounds, and cartoons appeared depicting misers in abandoned houses stuffed with hundreds of tires.

In such a time of confusion, with talk of the nation being forced to abandon civilian use of automobiles for the duration of the war, inventors stepped forward with plans for alternative sources of rubber. One idea involved extracting oil from garbage and soaking crude rubber in it. The rubber was supposed to double in size in 48 hours. It did, but the intense heat of the vulcanization process returned it to normal size. Other proposals urged that wheels be made from steel springs, or wood with asphalt rims.

Not all the confusion came from inventors with a loose wire upstairs. There were several ways to produce synthetic rubber; nobody could determine the best method in advance. To simplify greatly, synthetic rubber depended on styrene, a plastic readily available, and butadiene (pronounced bū-ta-dý-een). The latter could be made from petroleum or industrial alcohol (which could, in turn, be manufactured from any grain, or even potatoes). Farmers and the so-called farm bloc in the United States Senate favored a process which used farm products. The oil companies favored synthetic rubber made from petroleum.

Some charged that Standard Oil of New Jersey tried to foster the development of petroleum-based butadiene and retard use of alcohol-based rubber because of a potentially profitable agreement with a giant German chemical company, I.G. Farben, to share patents on petroleum-based products. In 1930, in Baton Rouge, Louisiana, a joint I. G. Farben-Standard Oil corporation, Jasco (Joint American Study Company) was established principally to develop petroleum-based synthetic rubber. The coming to power of Hitler in Germany did nothing to disturb Jasco. By 1936 Germany was producing in quantity a synthetic rubber based on industrial alcohol. In the United States, Standard Oil controlled the German rubber patents, but did little to create a demand for petroleum-based synthetic rubber. The formal dissolution of Jasco in late 1939 did not end the cooperative relationship between Standard and Farben. In early 1942 the Attorney General of the United States brought a giant anti-trust suit against Standard Oil. Charges of collaboration with the enemy were silenced at Roosevelt's order. He recognized the wartime value of Standard Oil for synthetic rubber production.

The synthetic rubber controversy relates not only to the recent energy crisis, but to a great dilemma of twentieth-century American society: the proper role of the federal government in regulating industrial production. In World War II, industry was allowed to do its job with little guidance from the federal government. New Deal agencies relaxed their supervision of business. The War Production Board, charged with the coordination of industry and government, believed that less federal regulation produced more industrial output. Critics argued that businessmen involved in one operation could not understand the overall war economy and therefore should not be depended upon for crucial technological choices.

The following discussions of the rubber problem by FDR and a major critic of the government's program raise significant questions about how the government ran the war. Can private business or independent observers be expected to understand and further the needs of a nation involved in total war? Was government best equipped to evaluate and coordinate war production? If speed is of the utmost importance, is it better to let private industry pick one plan and get to work even if the plan is not necessarily the best? What is the most sensible way to handle shortages in wartime? What right to criticize the government should the press enjoy in wartime? Did FDR act wisely in dealing with the rubber crisis?

SCRAP DRIVE—Throughout the spring of 1942 Franklin Roosevelt resisted his advisers who urged gasoline rationing to reduce rubber usage. The president hoped a less drastic measure might produce enough rubber. At last he hit upon a scheme. In the following nationwide radio broadcast on June 12, 1942, FDR announced plans for a drive to collect scrap rubber.[1]

I want to talk to you about rubber — about rubber and the war — about rubber and the American people.

When I say rubber, I mean rubber. I don't mean gasoline. Gasoline is a serious problem only in certain sections of the country.

But rubber is a problem everywhere — from one end of the country to the other — in the Mississippi Valley as well as in the East — in the oil country as well as in the corn country or the iron country or the great industrial centers.

Rubber is a problem for this reason — because modern wars cannot be won without rubber and because 92 percent of our normal supply of rubber has been cut off by the Japanese.

That is serious. It would be more serious if we had not built up a stock pile of rubber before the war started: if we were not now building up a great new synthetic rubber industry That takes time, so we have an immediate need.

Neither the stock pile, nor the synthetic plants which are now being built, nor both together, will be enough to provide for the needs of our great new army and navy plus our civilian requirements as they now exist.

The armed services have done what they can. They have eliminated rubber wherever possible. The army, for example, has had to replace rubber treads with less efficient steel treads on many of its tanks. Army and navy estimates of use of rubber have had to be curtailed all along the line.

But there is a limit to that.

You and I want the finest and most efficient army and navy the world has ever seen — an army and navy with the greatest and swiftest striking power. That means rubber — huge quantities of rubber — rubber for trucks and tanks and planes and gun mounts — rubber for gas masks and rubber for landing boats.

But it is not the army and navy alone which need rubber. The process of production also needs rubber. We need rubber to get our war workers back and forth to their plants — some of them far from workers' homes. We need rubber to keep our essential goods and supplies moving.

All this adds up to a very serious problem — a problem which is a challenge to the sound judgment of the government and to the ingenuity of the American people. It is a problem we Americans are laboring to solve — a problem we will solve.

But there is one unknown factor in this problem. We know what our stock pile is. We know what our synthetic capacity will be. But we do not know how much used rubber there is in the country — used rubber which, reclaimed and reprocessed, can be combined with our supplies of new rubber to make those supplies go farther in meeting military and civilian needs.

Specifically, we don't know how much used rubber there is in your cellar — your barn — your stock — your garage — your attic.

There are as many opinions as there are experts, and until we know we can't make our plans for the best use of the rubber we have.

The only way to find out is to get the used rubber in where it can stand up and be counted.

And that precisely is what we propose to do.

We are setting aside the two-week period from June 15 to June 30 — from 12:01 a.m., June 15, to 12 midnight, June 30 — to get the old rubber in.

We have asked the filling station operators — the thousands upon thousands of citizens who operate gas stations and garages from one end of the country to the other — to help. And they have generously and patriotically agreed to help: they and the oil companies which serve them.

They have agreed to take the old rubber in and to pay for it at the standard rate of a penny a pound — an amount which will later be refunded to them by the government.

I know that I don't need to urge you to take part in the collection drive. All you need to know is the place to take your rubber and the time to take it there — and the fact that your country needs it.

We do not want you to turn in essential rubber that you need in your daily life — rubber you will have to replace by buying new things in the store. We do want every bit of rubber you can possibly spare — and in any quantity — less than a pound — many pounds. We want it in every form — old tires, old rubber raincoats, old garden hose, rubber shoes, bathing caps, gloves — whatever you have that is made of rubber. If you think it is rubber, take it to your nearest filling station.

Once the rubber is in, we will know what our supplies of used rubber are and we will make our plans accordingly. One thing you can be sure of — we are going to see to it that there is enough rubber to build the planes to bomb Tokyo and Berlin — enough rubber to build the tanks to crush the enemy wherever we may find him — enough rubber to win this war.

Here are two simple rules for this rubber emergency.

1. Turn in all the old rubber — anywhere and everywhere.

2. Cut the use of your car — save its tires by driving slowly and driving less.

I know the nation will respond.

ANOTHER VIEW OF THE RUBBER CRISIS — The scrap rubber drive eventually collected about 450,000 tons of rubber, not nearly enough to meet the need. Furthermore, much of the scrap was not useable. The rubber shortage was widely debated in the press and by nationwide radio commentators, such as Fulton Lewis, Jr., who spoke five days a week over the Mutual Broadcasting System. Lewis, who started in radio in 1936, had achieved considerable notoriety as an isolationist opponent of Roosevelt's foreign policy before December 7, 1941. Lewis generally took the side of industry — in 1941 he was sponsored by the National Association of Manufacturers for a weekly series devoted to defense contractors. Once the war began, Lewis attacked problems of defense production; the numerous broadcasts he made regarding the synthetic rubber situation in the early summer of 1942 gave him a nationwide following.

Lewis presented a quantity of information, some of which was not quite accurate. He took up the rubber crisis with enthusiasm, convincing some members of Congress, as well as millions of his followers, that he had mastered the synthetic rubber problem. The following excerpts are from broadcasts made between June 19 and July 17, 1942.[2] In print, of course, the transcripts give no indication of Lewis' breathless delivery, his frequent innuendoes, or his hinting at dark conspiracies among unnamed Roosevelt appointees. Some claimed Lewis had a "voice with a snarl." At times he sounded a bit like Humphrey Bogart playing a particularly tough gangster. Lewis did not singlehandedly cause the July 20, 1942, passage of a bill designed to solve the rubber crisis, but he made an important contribution to demands for congressional action.

June 19, 1942

Regardless of dream ideas about workers bicycling to their jobs, the surest way to paralyze American war production is to fail to keep the nation on wheels. If all this rubber is needed by the war effort, it's even more serious. It means we actually will be short in providing the materials for war, let alone what happens here at home.

In either event, I am sure you will agree with one thing: that we need every possible pound of synthetic rubber we can get, as quickly as we can get it, and if there's any available source of it, the responsible government agencies here certainly should move heaven and earth to utilize every one of those sources.

And the whole gist of this story of mine is whether or not that is being done. . . .

The actual production of synthetic rubber is as simple as boiling potatoes on the back of the stove. It has two ingredients, which you mix together in an iron kettle or a washtub, or anything else, under a little pressure with a little heat, and you know you have synthetic rubber. It's literally as simple as that.

One of those ingredients is a straw-colored liquid called styrene, which comes from either petroleum or coal, and you can forget about that now, because there's no problem there. Plants that will produce the greatest abundance of styrene already are constructed, or under construction.

The other ingredient — and this is the one you should know about and remember, because this is the key to the whole thing — is a gas called butadiene, and it's the production of butadiene, to be used in that final simple process of making the synthetic rubber, that constitutes the whole problem.

There are two sources of butadiene. One is petroleum gases, and the process in that case is highly involved. It has some four or five steps, in which the natural petroleum gases are made into something else, and that's made into something else again, and so on, until you finally get the butadiene. The other source is alcohol, ordinary 190 proof industrial alcohol, about which you've heard so much, and there are several processes in that case, one of which has two steps, the other of which is a direct process. The alcohol is made into butadiene in one single step.

June 22, 1942

An engineer by the name of George Johnson — he's the head of the so-called little T. V. A. power project in Nebraska — has been trying to get permission to build a synthetic-rubber project in Nebraska. He has rounded up enough pumps — that's a major item in any of these plants — from deserted mines in Colorado; enough grain-grinding machinery from shut-down flour mills in the Wheat Belt; enough steam capacity from the reserve boilers of the power plants in Nebraska and adjoining states — boilers that were used an average of one hour in all of last year. He has options on vacant buildings or land adjoining those power plants. He has 90 percent enough material to set up a rubber plant to turn out 17,000 tons a year, and 50 percent enough material for 200,000 tons a year. All he needs for the 17,000-ton plant is 150 tons of steel reinforcing bars for concrete — that's for his fermentation vats, as substitutes for steel vats. While the other projects that have been authorized have been financed by the government, Mr. Johnson has his own private financing; he wants no loan or grant from the government — just 150 tons of steel, which is about one percent of the amount of steel that goes to the bottom of the Atlantic every time a cargo vessel is sunk — but neither the Rubber Reserve Company [the government agency in charge of synthetic rubber production] nor the War Production Board will permit him to go ahead.

Now, by way of one additional bit of background, you ought to understand that one of the oldest and bitterest feuds in all American industrial history has been the feud between the oil industry and alcohol. It's quite understandable — they're competitors in the world of fuels and in the world of chemicals — and that feud lies behind this whole controversy. The policymakers of the government on this synthetic-rubber picture are people who've lived all their lives with the petroleum side of that controversy. Some of them have had direct or indirect affiliations with the large oil companies themselves — others have affiliations with the large rubber companies, which, of course, have been arm in arm with the oil industry throughout the development of the automobile.

Now, let's pick up the story.

In this petroleum process a large part of the butadiene actually is to be made in the oil fields, because the petroleum industry wanted to keep it there; then, the butadiene is to be shipped to Akron, Ohio, where the rubber companies will do the actual manufacturing of the rubber. That requires special railroad tank cars, able to hold a pressure of 250 pounds, made of stainless steel, and lined with a special enamel; and more than 200 of them now are under construction.

The process that Mr. Johnson proposed was to take the grain at the place where the grain is, there turn it into alcohol, and there turn the alcohol into butadiene, and there turn the butadiene into rubber — all at the same place. . . .

I don't pretend to be any chemical engineer; but, for that matter, neither is Mr. Crossland [head of the Rubber Reserve Company]. He's an ex-bank examiner who has spent his whole life in finance and has been in the Reconstruction Finance Corporation since 1933, from which he was transferred to the Rubber Reserve Company. I have, however, been through more than a hundred of the largest industrial plants in America, of every kind and description, in the last year and a half — something Mr. Crossland has not done.

June 25, 1942

I've had a most astounding response from all over the nation on these broadcasts about the synthetic rubber picture — by long odds the most tremendous response I've ever had on any broadcast, or series of broadcasts, in all the five years I've been on the air. I've had literally thousands of letters and telegrams from you asking what you can do to help — telephone calls from California and Texas and everywhere in the country.

July 6, 1942

We have a sudden flare-up of activity in the synthetic-rubber picture tonight; as you know, I've been pounding away at this story for more than three weeks now; I felt rather lonely about it most of the time, but today, all of a sudden, things began happening on every side.

To begin with, five major oil companies published full page advertisements today in newspapers all over the nation announcing that they have a new process for making synthetic rubber far more quickly, far more economically, and in much greater quantity than any other petroleum process now under consideration. Those companies were Gulf, Standard Oil of New York, Standard of California — both of which are distinct from Standard of New Jersey, which has been involved in the synthetic-rubber picture to date — they have what is called the Houdry process, about which I'm trying to find out something for you, but I haven't the information tonight.

The other major development was even more important.

Mr. Donald Nelson, head of the War Production Board, appeared before a special investigating committee of Congress which has been looking into the facts that I presented to you about the synthetic-rubber production program, and in his typically sincere, straightforward manner, he took hold of the controversy with both hands, which is the first time that has been done.

First of all, Mr. Nelson told the Senate committee today that he has been placed in full and complete command of the rubber situation, which includes synthetic rubber production, and that means that there has been a sudden shake-up in this whole policy-making machinery in the last few days, because up until this time the Rubber Reserve Company has been in charge of it; in fact, the War Production Board tried to get full control early this year and was unable to do so. That much has been changed in the last few days.

July 16, 1942

Remember, ladies and gentlemen, this is all a question of whether the little people of America — not the big ones, because they'll be able to get tires somehow or other — it's the little ones who will have to go off wheels.

July 17, 1942

Now, I want to make a sort of final report to you this evening on this national rubber problem, with the understanding, of course, that whatever new developments occur from here on I'll present them to you as they happen.

It was just four weeks ago tonight that I gave you my first report on the subject, and at that time the picture was pretty black. Government officials, trying to make newspaper headlines, were telling you that American economy would have to go off wheels, that when existing tires were gone there'd be no more for civilians until the war is over. They said the army would have to put steel treads instead of rubber on tanks, thus reducing the speed considerably. Synthetic rubber was a national mystery; we didn't know what it was made of, or whether it was really practical or just a myth. We — you and I, as laymen — were caught in a crossfire of contradictions and semihysteria, and all sorts of extreme statements by government officials; none of us knew enough about it to know who was telling the truth, and that's why I went into it.

Since then a lot of water has gone over the dam. We've found out there isn't any great mystery about synthetic rubber. A special Senate committee has made an investigation, and Congress — your Congress — has taken a very strong hand in the picture. Four weeks ago the appointed officials in charge of this rubber program were coasting along glibly, having pretty much their own way, and you and I not knowing enough about the thing to know whether they were doing a competent, responsible job, or whether they weren't.

That is all ended.

A RESPONSE FROM ROOSEVELT — Responding in part to the radio broadcasts of Fulton Lewis, Jr., Congress passed a Rubber Supply Act on July 21, 1942. The bill called for congressional supervision of rubber production and directed that industrial alcohol, not petroleum, be used as the principal source of butadiene. The oil industry was outraged; Roosevelt feared the new agency would make coordination of industrial production (the goal of the War Production Board) impossible. The president's August 6, 1942, veto of the act, one of Roosevelt's strongest messages to Congress during the entire war, offered promise of immediate change.[3]

The approval of this bill would, in my opinion, block the

progress of the war production program and therefore the war itself.

The Congress of the United States has heretofore definitely laid down the policy, approved by the president, that in order to carry on a unified, integrated, and efficient program of war production it is necessary to centralize the power to determine the priorities of materials not only between military and civilian needs, but also among competing military needs. This power to fix priorities for the use of scarce materials has been vested by the Congress in the President of the United States, and has been delegated by him to the War Production Board. Experience in other wars, as well as in the present conflict, has proven beyond doubt that simplification of power with respect to the use of critical materials is essential to speed and efficiency. In fact, without this there can result only conflict and delay. . . .

This bill would immediately break up that logical coordination of centralized control, and would set up a new agency with the power and duty to manufacture alcohol and rubber, and to override all the priorities established by the War Production Board for materials necessary to manufacture all the other hundreds of products essential in war. It goes much further than that. It provides that even civilian needs of rubber — for pleasure driving, joy riding — must be given consideration, for the bill sets forth the duty of the new agency to furnish rubber in quantities sufficient "to meet the military and civilian needs of the United States" irrespective of the relationship of such civilian needs to winning the war.

The War Production Board has adopted a program for making synthetic rubber and is now operating under it. In doing so, it has endeavored to operate on the basis of estimated military needs for rubber and those civilian needs which are essential. By the phrase "essential needs" are meant those needs of civilians who require rubber in work directly related to the war effort — for example, driving to war-production plants in automobiles where other transportation is not readily available. It includes also certain necessities for the community, like getting milk to the consumer or children to school.

In order to produce any substantial amount of synthetic rubber, new plants must be constructed or old plants converted. In formulating its program, therefore, the War Production

Board has, of course, taken into consideration the amount of critical materials which can be diverted from other vital needs of the war program to build the plants to produce synthetic rubber.

In its program, the board has allocated a certain amount of rubber to be produced from agricultural products, and a certain amount to be made from petroleum. Both types of plants — those using farm products and those using petroleum — are now being constructed, and others are planned to be constructed month by month, at the greatest possible speed.

Every one of these plants and all the machinery to be installed in them will require large quantities of certain materials of which there is great scarcity and which are sorely needed for other war purposes. They will require steel plate, other steel, copper, bronze, and brass. Remember that every time steel plate is used for a synthetic rubber plant, just so much is being taken away from ships, tanks, high octane gasoline plants, and munitions plants. . . .

There is one other commodity — of supreme importance — which is involved in this question of synthetic rubber. That is food. The proposed bill not only provides for a complete supply of rubber for any and all purposes but it also directs that the new agency shall have the duty to "make available at the earliest possible time an adequate supply of alcohol produced from agricultural products to meet any military or civilian need of alcohol in the United States." In addition to the further consumption of critical materials for the construction of any new alcohol plants which the new agency may determine to be necessary, this provision may require the consumption of many millions of bushels of grain. Even the process of making synthetic rubber under the present program, now actually under way, will require almost 100,000,000 bushels of grain.

It is true that we have great grain reserves at present; but we must bear in mind that there is a steadily increasing demand for grain for the making of food for the army and navy and air force — not only of the United States but of all the United Nations. In the event of a serious drought next year like those of 1934 and 1936 — which is always a possibility — our reserves of grain may not be sufficient to cover the requirements both for food and for unlimited alcohol and rubber. Therefore the need of grain for food instead of unlimited rubber or alcohol is something which must also be taken into consideration by those charged with the over-all responsibility of the entire war-production effort.

The processes for making synthetic rubber are now in a state of flux. Some of them are in the purely experimental stage, others have been demonstrated to have varying degrees of efficiency. It was obviously impossible to determine in advance just which process will eventually prove to be the most desirable, taking into consideration the elements of speed, efficiency of production, and consumption of critical materials. . . . Determination in this more or less uncharted area should have the advantages of the flexibility of administrative action rather than be frozen by legislative mandate.

It may well be that serious mistakes have been made in the past, based either on misinformation, misconception, or even partiality to one process or another. It may be that the present program of the War Production Baord is not the best solution. If so, the facts should be ascertained and made public. This is particularly so, if it be true, as charged by some persons in the Congress and outside the Congress, that the manufacture of synthetic rubber from grain has been hamstrung by selfish business interests. . . .

In recent months there have been so many conflicting statements of fact concerning all the elements of the rubber situation — statements from responsible government agencies as well as from private sources — that I have set up a committee of three men to investigate the whole situation — to get the facts — and to report them to me as quickly as possible with their recommendations. . . . I am asking them to investigate the whole situation and to recommend such action as will produce the rubber necessary for our total war effort, including essential civilian use, with a minimum interference with the production of other weapons of war.

The Baruch committee, composed of Bernard Baruch, chairman; Dr. James B. Conant, president of Harvard University; and Dr. Karl Compton, president of the Massachusetts Institute of Technology, worked quickly and presented a public report in a matter of weeks. As a result, William M. Jeffers, president of the Union Pacific Railroad, was appointed rubber director (he was commonly referred to as the rubber "czar") September 15, 1942. Jeffers rejected the proposals of the farm bloc for alcohol-based synthetic rubber, instead relying principally on the major oil companies for petroleum-based butadiene. By the time he resigned, one year later, the crisis was over. In 1944 more than enough synthetic rubber was produced at home. Since 1945 rubber production in the United States has continued to be based primarily on petroleum-based synthetic materials.

Those, who in May 1942 claimed that no civilian would drive his car again for the duration of the war, were proved wrong. Thanks to one of the great "miracles" of American industrial genius, the rubber problem was solved. Not always acknowledged is the debt the rubber industry owes to German technology. Americans learned of the developments in synthetic rubber by visiting Germany of the 1920s and 1930s. Today's principal synthetic rubber is a refinement of the synthetic rubber manufactured in World War II, which is a refinement of the German buna-type rubbers. The "miracle" in America was in mass production, not rubber technology. This is not to belittle American polymer science; it takes more than laboratory expertise to produce millions of tires in a matter of months. Yet during the war and for some time after, it seemed patriotically necessary to deny any German role in synthetic rubber. It is no longer necessary to be so chauvinistic.

Notes

1. Samuel I. Rosenman, ed., *The Public Papers and Addresses of Franklin D. Roosevelt: 1942* (New York, 1950), 270-273.
2. *Congressional Record*, 77th Congress, Second Session, Volume 88, Part 5, 6754-64.
3. *Ibid.*, 6752-53.

Women war workers (and male supervisors) in a west coast air-craft plant. [National Archives Photo.]

CHAPTER TEN

For the Duration: Women in War Industries

MARY ANDERSON, MARY ELIZABETH PIDGEON,
and MARGARET HICKEY

Introduction by
JOANNA SCHNEIDER ZANGRANDO

World War II was not the first time that thousands of American women responded to emergency demands to join the industrial work force. Early in the nineteenth century, young women and girls relieved the labor scarce economy by becoming New England textile mill operatives, freeing men for agricultural production. Women demonstrated both skill and patriotism in assuming a variety of industrial occupations during the Civil War and World War I. However, the assumption persisted that women's participation in the paid work force was temporary, until the end of a particular national emergency. Spokesmen for industry, government, organized labor, and the public media believed that the proper role for women, regardless of their economic needs, individual competence, personal preferences, or marital status, was that of homemaker. Economic opportunities for women were sharply proscribed, and any deviations evoked the arguments that a woman's "natural" roles were those of wife and mother, that women worked only for "pin money," that they took jobs away from male breadwinners, and that women could not perform difficult, tedious, and heavy factory tasks satisfactorily. Such opinions provided justification for outright discrimination against women. Approximately one million women worked in a variety of factory jobs by 1890, but they were segregated into "women's jobs," demanding little skill, carrying low wages, and offering negligible opportunities for advancement. Even labor unions proved reluctant to recruit women and to upgrade their work status.

That government, industry, union, and public media spokesmen expected women to fit neatly into the industrial defense effort during World War II on a temporary, emergency basis seems evident in their recruitment slogan, "For the Duration." Despite magnanimous praise for the indispensable role women played in the war effort, an emphasis on patriotic duty indicated that with victory assured, women's next duty would be to make way for returning veterans, relinquish their industrial jobs, and return to their homes. Few training programs led to skilled jobs and promotions. During the war, only 10 percent of the needed child care facilities were actually provided. Wartime union agreements contained equal wage rates for women and men doing the same work in the same plants. Yet, union contracts for the hiring of married women allowed separate seniority lists and the furloughing of such women before males or single females.

What did women do? They responded by the thousands to the calls to serve the war effort. With speed and skill they shouldered industrial tasks denied them only months before as too taxing and complicated. Miraculously, they juggled long, tiring hours on assembly lines with home responsibilities that had no time limits and carried no reimbursements. While participating in the paid work force, they demonstrated that long-standing stereotypes and proscriptions imposed upon women ignored reality: women — including older women with children — performed admirably in skilled, high-paying jobs. Furthermore, they intended to remain as permanent members of the industrial work force. The participation of women in the paid work force increased from 13 million in 1940 to over 19 million by the end of 1944.

Before World War II, the majority of women workers had been young and single. But the war emergency set in motion a counter trend that has continued to the present. From 1940 to 1970, the participation of married women in the labor force almost tripled, from 14 percent in 1940 to 40 percent in 1970. In addition, an increasing number of older women joined and continued in the work force: 15 percent of married women between 35 and 44 years old (with husbands present in the home) were working in 1940, 46 percent in 1970; 11 percent of such women between 45 and 54 years old worked in 1940, 48 percent in 1970; and seven percent of women between 55 and 64 years old were workers in 1940, 35 percent in 1970. Women either have chosen or have been forced by economic need to enter and to remain in the paid work force in ever increasing numbers since 1940.

The following documents, concerned with the paid work of women in war-related industries and professions, reflect the perspectives of strategically placed women in the federal government. These women officials knew, both as participants in and observers of women's contributions to the paid work force, that capable and enthusiastic women continued to suffer from sex-stereotyping and discrimination, regardless of their service to the nation. They articulated the concerns of millions of women wage earners: the right to work at good jobs, under safe conditions, for equitable pay, and with access to training and promotion opportunities for as long as they wished to work.

In reading what follows, consider these questions: How valid was the argument that industrial jobs were too heavy, tedious, and complicated for most women? Why was this argument used? Did the government and industry view women merely as a reserve labor force to be used in emergencies and then dismissed? Did women consciously intend to challenge this view? What effect did participation in the war effort have on the economic and social attitudes and status of American women?

JOBS FOR WOMEN— Mary Anderson's appraisal of the contributions of women wage earners to the defense effort was based on Women's Bureau studies of war industries throughout the United States, and years of first-hand experience in industry and the trade union movement. Born in Sweden in 1872, she came to the United States at the age of 16. She first worked in a garment factory, then as a machine operator in a shoe factory, where she became president of a union local. Anderson left to become an organizer for the National Women's Trade Union League. During World War I she supervised government studies of working conditions for women in munitions plants. When the temporary wartime organization she headed was converted to the permanent Women's Bureau in 1920, Mary Anderson assumed the position of director.

The Women's Bureau set employment standards for women and published data on their working conditions. The bureau underscored Anderson's contentions that women worked because of economic need, and not for "pin money;" that women were capable, crucial, and permanent contributors to the industrial work force; and that sex discrimination not only was unfair, but also was economically wasteful.

In a March 1942 speech, Anderson described the situation confronting American women as increasing numbers entered the work force.[1]

The time has passed when an employer could depend solely on men to fill his work benches and his drafting tables; no more can he believe that the labor supply of men is plentiful or that he can hire it away from some competitor at a higher wage. And, of course, the time is long past when jobs in factories can be described as requiring a strong back and a weak mind. I saw a news item the other day where someone said that the delicate essentials of airplane construction can be done very well by women, at the sacrifice only of long fingernails.

There has been an overnight shift in women's position; the sudden entrance of the country into war has moved them from the second line of defense workers to the front line. . . .

Women are not yet employed as extensively as war workers as they are in factory work in peacetime. By war workers I mean those employees who have been added to the labor force of the country, in whatsoever capacity, because of the war-production program. . . . The Women's Bureau made some surveys last year of defense industries, and now we are checking on the progress made in the employment of women since that time. For example, the following story of how one company took care to place women most efficiently is of great interest:

In April an airplane assembly plant as an experiment employed 16 girls and placed some of them in the covering and paint departments, others in electrical assemblies. The experiment was so successful that at the end of the year they were employing 500 women, but also they were utilizing women in nearly all productive processes throughout the plant, including the machine shop, and even on the final assembly. Most of the jobs on which they start the girls in this plant take only a few days of breaking-in, and then the girls are upgraded through in-plant training and supplementary courses. However, about 80 or 90 percent of the girls had had either factory experience in other industries or pre-employment training. The plant has these courses 24 hours a day, and all are open to women. In addition to other courses, some are taking riveting and sheet-metal work. (This is the only plant visited by the Women's Bureau to date where all in-plant courses are open to women.)

This is the plant whose total employment rose from 1,255 at the beginning of 1940 to 4,500 by the end of 1940, with no women employed at all, and in January 1942 there were over 500 women out of the 6,000 total employed. . . .

The aircraft plants in this country employ only an infinitesimal proportion of women, whereas in England they comprise 40 to 50 percent of the workers. In small-arms ammunition 40 percent of the workers in this country are women, compared to 80 percent in Wales.

What are prospects for women being readily absorbed into the rapidly expanding production program? In the first place, new jobs have been created through the break-down of big processes into the simpler and less skilled operations. The phenomenal need for more workers to produce more fighting equipment makes mandatory a job analysis to break down certain processes so that they will be within the reach of the great potential woman labor supply. . . .

These jobs constitute a sort of no man's land in regard to occupation and sex. They are restricted by no traditions as to whether they should be done by men or women. To draw hard and fast lines between men's and women's jobs is out of the question. The recruitment of women is easier than that of men simply because there is a larger volume of women ready to be hired. . . .

Some jobs can be done equally well by men or women, such as milling machines; light punch and forming presses; bench and watchmakers' lathes; burring, polishing, lapping, buffing — on lathes; packing, labeling. Some jobs can be done even better by women because of certain peculiarly feminine qualifications; painstaking, tedious work requiring greater patience, finger dexterity. Women adapt themselves readily to repetitive jobs requiring constant alertness if not skill, strong fingers and tireless wrists, with no flagging. Examples are: drill presses; assembly — all types; winding coils and armatures; soldering; taping; painting — all kinds (spray, stencil, radium, touch-up); visual inspection.

But women can do certain notably skilled work, after training. Women have the ability to work to precise tolerances, can detect variations of ten-thousandths of an inch. Women can make careful adjustments at high speed with great accuracy. Illustrations of such skill are: welding, sheet metal forming and riveting; light turret lathes; light-duty hand and automatic screw machines; setting-up machines; production, planning, routing, tracing, drafting. . . In aircraft assembly, one-fourth to one-third of the jobs might be filled by women. . . .

In contrast to the aircraft industry, the plants making ammunition for small arms and for artillery already employ large numbers of women. . . . In the mechanical time-fuze department of a government arsenal, three years ago only two percent of the workers were women, now 96 percent are women, and more fuzes are being produced per employee than ever before. There has been a complete change in the breakdown of operations. . . .

Women have been definitely handicapped by lack of training. So is anyone — but my point is that the vocational-training courses have not been opened to women as readily as to men, and in some important cases, not opened to them at all. . . . Of 1,778,000 persons given training in the vocational training classes for national defense, since the beginning of the program in July 1940, about 17,000 were women (less than one percent). These figures are up to December 1, 1941, and since then presumably more women are admitted. The National Youth Administration has trained women up to 25 years of age for defense industries, and the Work Projects Administration has given training to some women. I am talking, of course, not about sewing power-machine-operator courses or cooking or nurses' aid training — but training in metal work, in electrical assembly, and the like.

It seems to us that there should be a more noticeable trend toward hiring older women, for dropping the bars against women in their late 30's, or even in their 40's. Some of these have had excellent industrial experience. A California Department of Employment report shows that some employers were of the opinion that the upper age limit would be extended to 40 or even 45 years of age, and in this survey there was found to be no noticeable increase or decrease in productivity in relation to age although the companies generally believed that women over 35 would be less desirable workers than the younger women. Conditions now are not peacetime normal conditions — the middle-aged woman whose experience and adaptability demonstrate fitness should be hired.

Most recent reports from our current visits to plants indicate that pre-employment training is not considered necessary for the jobs women are being hired for, and I look to immediate widespread hiring of women for the so-called first jobs in the factories, the simpler semiskilled ones. If women are to progress and be effectively employed, they should not be restricted to the least skilled jobs, and we want to see supplementary training opened to them. All aircraft manufacturing centers have training programs for men, for example, but only in one plant — of all those visited by the Women's Bureau to date — do we know that all the supplementary courses are open to women, that they can enter any course they choose. We would like to see women taught the related skills, such as blueprint reading, shop mathematics, speeds and needs of cutting tools, use of scales and micrometers. Our recent visits to plants show that women are taking blueprint reading wherever such courses are open to them; other courses chosen by them are, machine shop, sheet metal, riveting, drafting. . . .

I want to emphasize the availability of trained professional women for plant jobs other than the production-line jobs. A news item the other day said that electrical manufacturing companies are asking for women college graduates who have concentrated in mathematics, chemistry, or physics, to serve as assistant engineers for work on estimates and mathematical computations, some women also will be able to find positions as radio physicists and technicians. A large manufacturing concern wanted a woman college graduate trained in mathematics to teach shop mathematics to mechanics who are taking in-service training.

Some of the engineering schools of the universities are opening their defense training courses to women. The courses qualify women for positions as draftsmen, inspectors, supervisors, engine testing, computation, and a wide range of precision work. There were, in November 1941, 4,436 women enrolled in these courses in 124 colleges and universities.

Supervision of women presents no different problems than supervision of men, but if the foreman resents the introduction of women into the plant — be it conscious or unconscious on his part — or if the men themselves dislike the presence of women in the once monastic atmosphere, there is not likely to be that smoothness or efficiency that results in adequate production. Certainly the personnel officials, and management itself, should be aware of any attitudes that would hinder the plant's highest efficiency.

A California survey, made by the California Department of Employment, of plants employing women in war production showed that as a whole men and women employees worked satisfactorily together. In all the plants surveyed, men and women were employed on the same job at the same rate of pay, very often working side by side. One employer preferred to have the men and women work together and believed that the women's higher rate of production would result in an increase in the men's rate of production. In some, it was found that the men employees had at first resented the employment of women, ridiculing the idea and working with the women only in a condescending manner. In one plant resentment on the part of the various supervisors was the most formidable obstacle in introducing women workers; these men had not previously supervised women and at first found it disagreeable. Within a short time the men who were in charge of women workers agreed that they were at least as easy to supervise as were men. The men workers felt women should be employed on the less skilled jobs, small-machine operations, and inspection, and resented the employment of women on machines requiring unusual mechanical ability. Of course, the theory that "women have no mechanical ability, interest, or aptitude" was exploded in the last world war. . . .

We believe that it is important to have a woman personnel official on the administrative staff. In some plants we have visited, a woman is in charge of personnel matters where women employees are concerned or plans are under way to employ one as soon as the extra numbers of women are hired. But in others there is only a matron or so-called hostess in charge of the women's service rooms; these act as counselors to the girls in some plants.

Working conditions are good in the plants we have visited. The Women's Bureau recommends the eight-hour day, with three shifts if necessary. We recommend that wage rates for women, including the entrance rates, be equal to those for men workers. As to night work, we believe investigation of each plant wanting to use women on a night shift should be made by the proper state authorities to determine whether there is a real need for such employment. We believe such permission should be granted only for the duration of the war. . . .

Employers who decide to hire women for the first time are in some instances perturbed as to the need to make plant adjustments to women's needs. I do not feel it necessary to make comment on this; practically all plants being built now have provided service facilities for women, or can easily convert plant space for them. Some employers, we find, are waiting to add extra facilities until the extra numbers of women are hired. Only in one plant was the premium on plant space so great that adding service facilities for more women seems a deterring factor on their greater employment. . . .

Since women have become such an important part of the nation's labor force for war production, the Women's Bureau realizes that for managements hiring women for the first time certain problems are bound to arise under the many differing circumstances. Therefore, we stand ready at all times to advise individual employers and plant officials as to occupations, standards, policies, and procedures to promote women's efficiency and to safeguard their health as workers.

PROGRESS OF WOMEN WORKERS — Two years after Mary Anderson's survey, Mary Elizabeth Pidgeon, chief of the Women's Bureau research division, reviewed the progress that had been made and pointed to questions which concerned women war workers.[2]

In the past the opportunity given women workers to learn and to exercise skills has been narrower in range than men's has been. In consequence, very large numbers of women were little thought of in connection with other types of work, and so they continued to be given little opportunity to develop additional skills. The war situation has changed that considerably. With shortages of men workers, women have been employed in a greater variety of occupations than before. Thus they have been given new opportunities to acquire and to develop additional skills. . . .

Unfortunately, there are many cases where women still have been given far too little chance to be upgraded to their highest skills. In 1943, the National Industrial Conference Board analyzed reports from some 130 plants, chiefly in heavier metal industries, plants that had employed relatively few women or none. In nearly 60 percent of these plants there were no plans for advancing women from the top production jobs they held at the time of reporting to more highly skilled jobs. Moreover, numerous instances are reported of the placement of women in jobs that are not in the usual line for the job progression; in such blind-alley jobs neither proficiency nor length of service can bring these women beyond a limited early stage of work. If this situation continues, it will be a great disadvantage to women after the war, and in fact government agencies are finding promotional discrimination against them as one of the major reasons why women quit jobs in war plants. Whether or not this continues may depend largely on the length of the war and the consequent stringency in the labor supply. It also will depend to some extent on how proficient women show themselves to be. . . .

That . . . difficulties also beset women in other fields is shown in the experience of professional women in their efforts to progress toward their best service. For example, it was not until a year and a half after Pearl Harbor that a law was passed permitting women doctors to be commissioned in the U.S. Army and Navy. At least one outstanding woman specialist had long previously tendered her services to Great Britain, where she was accorded rank more appropriate to her abilities. In mid-1943, the president of the National Federation of Business and Professional Women's Clubs stated in convention:

> I solemnly charge that the war is being slowed down here in America by the failure of the government and private enterprise alike to use women's brains and training in their specialized fields.

The appreciation of the work women have been doing has been widespread. In August 1943, on the first anniversary of the army order to replace draft-age men with women wherever possible, Under Secretary of War Robert P. Patterson stated:

> The women of America have responded ably and gallantly to the call to service the war has made upon them. Nowhere is this more evident than in the plants operated by the War Department. They have supplanted men at the bench and the lathe; they are doing civilian work in the nine Service Commands efficiently and in increasing numbers.
>
> In the arsenals, in the ports of embarkation, in the motor centers, in all the War Department installations, their skills are invaluable and their devotion to duty is proven. They are testing guns, making ammunition, fixing motors, sewing uniforms, inspecting ordnance, driving trucks, doing many of the thousand and one jobs that are necessary to keep the machinery of war moving.
>
> I salute them for their faithfulness, their cheerful courage, and their patriotism. . . .

At any period of job shortages, the seniority status that workers have been able to develop greatly influences their chances of employment. The many women recent entrants to the labor market naturally have not yet built up long seniority records. Their chances will be limited sharply in the face of men who return with longer records. . . . Many plants have arranged for an automatic extension of seniority for their permanent workers called to war services and afterward returning to the plant. For example, a study of some 250 companies showed that nine-tenths of them provide full continuous-service credit for employees on military leave. . . .

Plant seniority practices under the clauses of many union agreements give women workers very inadequate protection. For example, some agreements definitely provide that women's occupation of jobs formerly held by men shall be for the duration only. Some agreements give women employed at time of signing the agreement full seniority rights with men, but for women employed after that time set up a list for women separate from that for men. Some agreements provide for the seniority of women as "separate and distinct from the seniority of men." Agreements fixing seniority by department only may affect women and men quite differently. Other agreements are so vaguely worded as to permit interpretations that are of disadvantage to women.

Among special sufferers from lack of seniority may be large numbers of married women who have responded in good faith to their country's call to war production. In many cases such workers may desire to leave their industrial jobs. But it must not be forgotten that there are numerous instances in which their financial assistance is needed by the families, and the aftermath of war is likely to add to this number. An example of their probable treatment in too many cases is illustrated by recent amendments to the unemployment compensation act in one state that provides that plants formerly having a rule barring married women from employment may reinstate this rule immediately after the war. Married women workers of these plants will at once lose their jobs, and probably will not be eligible to receive unemployment insurance to tide them over this transition period in their lives.

The extent of this problem may be indicated from a sample of 35 ordnance, aircraft, and other war industry plants, in half of which at least 50 percent of the woman labor force were married. Some employers took on married women by preference, with the idea that when lay-offs came the husband would be a wage earner and the wife could go. But many of these male wage earners may not return, or may be disabled, and it cannot be assumed that these married women can automatically return home.

WOMEN IN A TRANSITION ECONOMY — At the end of 1944, Margaret Hickey applauded the contributions of women to wartime production. Hickey had been appointed in 1942 to head the Woman's Advisory Committee of the War Manpower Commission 14 women who represented a geographic, management, labor, and general public cross section. The committee prepared guidelines on ending discrimination against women in defense industries, and offered suggestions on the best allocation and utilization of women in those industries. Hickey brought to the committee years of experience and effort on behalf of professional women. Although admitted to the Missouri bar in 1928, she established a secretarial training

school and became a leader in the vocational guidance
movement in Missouri. In 1944 she served as president of the
National Federation of Business and Professional Women's
Clubs. From her vantage point of professional experience and
wartime government service, Hickey warned in December
1944 that vigilance must be maintained during reconversion to
a peacetime economy lest women lose the economic gains of
the war years.[3]

Women have done a magnificent job in the war. The overall
manpower picture remains satisfactory, and the more than
18,000,000 working women make up well over a third of it.
Without women the almost staggering production records to
date would have been impossible.

It will be a sad commentary on our democratic institutions
if after the war women are treated merely as competitors for
jobs. Under the Selective Service Act, men of the armed forces,
of course, will have their old jobs back. But returning veterans
cannot be counted upon for the support of all feminine
members of their respective households. Regardless of marital
status, the majority of women who work do so out of economic
necessity.

There are many who in theory admit women's full right to
work. But in practice it has been noted that whenever
unemployment threatens to appear on the surface of economic
life, the right of women to work is always brought under attack.
Danger signals are appearing on the horizon of postwar planning
now. Some are discussing the demobilization of women,
particularly married women, as though the object were to deny
them employment regardless of their need to earn a living.

The depression restrictions set up in this country to drive
women out of employment regardless of their economic need
served to hide, but did not eliminate unemployment. And it is
well to remember also that prejudices surrounding the employment of women have been shuffled around considerably during
the war, but they have not been eliminated.

The women of America formed a hidden army upon which
Hitler in his madness failed to count. That once hidden army of
women is now in the open. We must face it realistically and
guard against the creation of another "hidden" army of
unemployed.

The best way to prevent the re-erection of pre-war barriers to women's employment is to keep the demand for labor so high that the help of every worker is needed. To put it another way, we must achieve a high level of production and a broad scale of distribution. In our effort toward these objectives, we should strive to make and keep the labor standards high.

The War Manpower Commission's Women's Advisory Committee, at its first meeting on October 1, 1942, formulated some basic recommendations which the War Manpower Commission accepted as policy. These called for the removal of all barriers to the employment of women in any occupation for which they were or could be fitted; for the admission of women on a basis of equality with men to all forms of training; and for the determination of wage rates on the basis of work performed irrespective of sex.

The opposition of the committee to discrimination in employment on the basis of sex in time of war or peace was elaborated on in a statement sent early in 1944 to Bernard M. Baruch, Advisory Unit for War and Post-War Adjustment Policy, Office of War Mobilization. In March of this year the Committee recommended a five-point program for application to women workers during the period of reconversion.

Since 1942, the War Labor Board has made several important decisions in favor of equal pay for comparable work. A few thousand firms and many union contracts have equalized wage rates for hundreds of thousands of women, but the universal acceptance of equal pay in fact is a goal yet to be achieved.

In the shifts and changes of the reconversion period, when women will be released from jobs where they have had equality of pay, there is danger of a return to prewar inequalities. There will be a tendency for the inexperienced and unskilled women workers to accept lower wages and therefore undermine the wage structure.

Inequalities in pay promote price cutting, depress the market, and unbalance the whole economic system. Practice of the equality principle protects the job opportunities of all qualified men and women.

Today only five states — Montana, Michigan, Washington, Illinois and New York — have equal pay laws. Thirty-nine of the 43 states lacking such statutes will hold regular legislative sessions in 1945. Representatives of 20 national women's organizations met in New York recently to discuss procedures for waging local campaigns for legislation to abolish the practice of sex discrimination in the payment of wages.

Only through positive and specific planning for the placement of individual workers and for the determination of wages on the basis of merit and regardless of sex can maximum efficiency in our industrial structure be assured and harmony in social relationships achieved.

Mary Anderson's confident predictions of women's capabilities in defense production proved absolutely correct. So, too, did Margaret Hickey's observation that prejudices against women workers had merely "been shuffled around," not ended.

Once the wartime crisis passed, policy-makers in government, in labor unions, in business and industry failed to move beyond their traditional views of women as homemakers who did not need to work. Since men in positions of authority refused to recognize women as a permanent part of the paid work force, discrimination against female workers ultimately resulted in widespread dismissals of women workers after the war. By November 1946 employers had dropped more than two million women from their payrolls. The unwillingness or inability to make any real commitment to postwar job equity and enhanced economic status for women meant that the achievement of such goals would await agitation by women in the work force and their allies in the years ahead.

NOTES

1. *Congressional Record*, 77th Congress, Second Session, Volume 88, Part 8, A1213-15.
2. "A Preview as to Women Workers in Transition from War to Peace" Special Bulletin Number 18 of the Women's Bureau, G.P.O., March, 1944.
3. National Women's Trade Union League, *Life and Labor Bulletin*, December, 1944.

Franklin Roosevelt and Joseph Stalin at the Yalta Conference, February 1945. [U.S. Army Signal Corps photo]

CHAPTER ELEVEN

FDR and World Affairs

ADOLF A. BERLE

Introduction by DAVID E. KYVIG

Adolf Berle was generally conceded to be one of the most brilliant people ever to serve in the administration of Franklin D. Roosevelt. An early advisor on economic matters, Berle probably made his greatest contribution to FDR's government in foreign affairs. As Assistant Secretary of State from 1938 to 1944, Berle participated in many crucial policy decisions of World War II and in particular helped shape American policy toward Latin America.

Adolf A. Berle, Jr., born in Chicago January 29, 1895, was the son of a Congregational minister who was active in social reform movements. Something of a child prodigy, Berle obtained his B.A. in 1913 at the age of 18, a master's degree the following year, and his law degree in 1916, all from Harvard. He joined Louis Brandeis' Boston law firm, then enlisted in the army at the outbreak of World War I. As an officer, he was sent to Santo Domingo to help increase sugar production — the beginning of a lifelong involvement with Latin America — and later served as an expert on Russian economics. Berle was sent to the 1919 Versailles peace conference as a member of an army staff of experts. He became disillusioned with the peacemaking and League of Nations because of the exclusion of Germany and the Soviet Union from both. With several others, he resigned his position before the conference ended.

Thereafter, Berle practiced law in New York City, worked at the Henry Street Settlement House for three years, taught corporation finance at the Harvard Business School, 1924-1927, and, in 1927, became professor of law at Colum-

bia University. While at Columbia, Berle, assisted by economist
Gardiner C. Means, wrote an enormously influential book, *The
Modern Corporation and Private Property* (New York, 1932).
In brief, Berle and Means pointed out that the classic free
market economy had disappeared, that individually-owned enterprise was being replaced primarily by large corporations financed by stockholders and profit, and that control of corporations had passed from the owners to the managers. Managers
of giant corporations had only symbolic responsibility to the
diffuse body of stockholders and none toward the workers or
the community. Furthermore, corporations had outgrown the
checks of supply and demand, enabling them to manipulate the
economy. According to Berle and Means, corporations had become social institutions requiring greater governmental control
so that society could share their benefits and be spared their
dangers. The book, vastly more sophisticated than can be indicated here, had a deep and lasting effect on American economic
thought.

Berle was asked to join Franklin Roosevelt's "Brain Trust"
in 1932. With Rexford Tugwell and Raymond Moley, he provided economic advice, proposed legislation, and wrote campaign speeches for the presidential candidate. Unlike the other
Brain Trusters, however, Berle did not immediately accept a
full-time position in the Roosevelt administration. He did help
draft legislation during the Hundred Days Congress, he served
as general counsel for the Reconstruction Finance Corporation, and on an intermittent basis, FDR sought his advice on
economic matters. For the most part he remained in New
York, where he developed a close association with Fiorello
LaGuardia and became city chamberlain, chief administrator,
for the nominally Republican mayor.

In 1938, Berle, who had rejected earlier federal job offers,
accepted the position of Assistant Secretary of State. After
five months he sought to resign, but Roosevelt urged him to
continue because of the difficult world situation. He remained
at the post for six years. Berle concerned himself with Latin
American and hemispheric defense, with an international
agreement governing civil aviation, and perhaps most of all,
with keeping peace between his continually quarrelsome supe-
riors, Secretary of State Cordell Hull and Undersecretary
Sumner Welles. More than ever before, Berle dealt with the
president on a regular, frequent basis during the war years.
When Hull retired near the end of 1944, Berle accepted the
ambassadorship to Brazil, a position he held until February
1946.

After his resignation from government service, Berle returned to teaching, writing, and lecturing. He served as chairman of the New York State Liberal Party from 1947 to 1955, but continued to be active in Democratic circles as well. His interest in Latin America remained intense, and he served as chairman of John F. Kennedy's Task Force on Latin America. He later advised Lyndon Johnson during the 1965 Santa Domingo crisis. His ceaseless activity ended on February 17, 1971, when he died shortly after his seventy-sixth birthday.

In a May 26, 1965, speech at Kalamazoo College, Adolf Berle discussed Franklin Roosevelt's conduct of American foreign relations as well as FDR's style of leadership and the president's image during and after his lifetime. Berle gave Roosevelt high marks as a politician and diplomat.

While reading the text consider a series of questions. Are Berle's standards for evaluating FDR reasonable, or is he too admiring of compromise and manipulation? Did the president act wisely in dealing with the Nazi collaborator Admiral Darlan? Did Roosevelt handle the Yalta Conference wisely? Berle was concerned with the variety of images of an historical figure during and after his lifetime and with the use of an image to influence events. Does his view of how historical images develop and exert influence make sense? Was FDR foolish to depend on the force of his own image to uphold the Yalta agreements? Has Roosevelt's image changed significantly since his death? If so, how and why? If not, why not?

I am perfectly clear that what Franklin Roosevelt really had most on his mind was how to get the job done, how to get from here where we all were towards there, where we all hoped to be. Now in foreign affairs he had a vast conception, indeed, a vast dream. That dream is in doubt today. He was seeking a world of law, a world which would acknowledge law. He was seeking a world of peace which would move through processes of peace. He was seeking a world which would develop by social evolution rather than by the endless force processes which have disfigured history. This is not a simple thing to do. The world has been around a long time and human nature for quite a large part of that time. So an endeavor to work out instincts around which could gather the slow force of institutional tradition was thinking on very large lines indeed. He considered that the world must be available in greater degree to the humblest laborer in Kalamazoo, Michigan, or Belgrade, Yugoslavia, or Rio de Janeiro, not merely to students of political literature, much as he respected scholarship. It was the result that counted.

Now in the Department of State, where I then worked as assistant secretary in varying ranks, we occasionally discussed this world which President Roosevelt had thrown out in the Atlantic Charter and in the Four Freedoms and in the three or four addresses he made on war objectives. As I say, in the Department of State where frequently you are on the firing line, we discussed these conceptions. We discussed the world we hoped would come out of them with a quiet, courteous, battle-scarred realist who was then Secretary of State, Mr. Cordell Hull of Tennessee. Cordell Hull would never let us get very far. He brought us back to our nuts and bolts with an acid comment. He used to say "Gentlemen, it is grand to be in heaven. But the question is how do you get there?" With that savage reminder we were back to drafting our documents and day-to-day decisions.

For the progress toward any stated political objective is actually accomplished not in great and sweeping moves. Once in awhile something has happened, and you can embody it in a magnificent document and gesture. It actually is the result of an endless mass of swift decisions on detail required by a brutal beltline of incoming people, papers, and problems carrying their questions and their demands for decision in an implacable volume. Your decision is: shall this problem be met or ducked and left aside, or shall it be dealt with thus and so? Shall this request be accepted, that one denied? Will you accept this pressure though you do not agree with it or will you resist it up to the point where politically you endanger something else? Should someone be sent to a trouble spot, and if so, what is he expected to do when he gets there? What shall be publicly said about each of these decisions, or the ones worth commenting on, as this endless driving ribbon of events continues to the point where your eyes are tired and your brain reels and you sleep, not because you think you have the right to, but because without it the next day's work will be even fuzzier than the last. This is what government work is, especially government in wartime. It is what crisis government is. And this was crisis government practically from the time President Roosevelt assumed office to the time of his death.

Now I'd like to take two illustrations of what happened. One of them was a success. The second one was a failure. The first relates to the famous expedition into the Mediterranean which took North Africa in 1943. What had happened there, you see, was that France had surrendered. They had made the famous armistice, and the Vichy government, emerging from the fall of France in 1941, was ruling France under an armistice with the Germans. The North African provinces, as they once were colonies of France, were occupied by French armies. These armies were still under the orders of Marshall [Henri Philippe] Pétain, [Premier Pierre] Laval, and the Vichy government. The total of the French-held territories was, at that point, nearly a third of the land mass of Africa, running all the way from Dakar clear over to Tunis. And we, in the war since Pearl Harbor, had not had time to build up the massive forces which would be needed to conduct a direct invasion of France, throwing the Germans out of France, though Stalin pressed bitterly for such an invasion. It would have helped him, and in retrospect one suspects that he would have been quite philosophical if it had also meant disaster for us. He was thinking as men will under those circumstances. One need not even accuse him of being insincere. He was thinking, of course, of his own people and his own country and his own fortunes. And having at that point been able to get approximately eight disposable divisions, which were not nearly enough for that, we considered other alternatives. It was finally proposed in Washington, in my library one evening, that an expedition would be sent to attack Africa, throwing the war back into the Mediterranean, relieving at least Egypt and the British-held countries in the eastern Mediterranean from the then joint Italian-German attack, and giving us a chance to force the war back towards the enemy instead of merely defending as it came closer towards Great Britain and to ourselves.

North Africa, as I said, was then held by the Vichy French army. Nobody particularly liked the idea of recognizing Vichy authority. Churchill wanted to recognize [Brigader General Charles] deGaulle [head of the "Free French" government-in-exile] and make it a deGaulle operation. I was asked to make explorations of deGaulle's personal following and strength in North Africa and did so, and there was none. DeGaulle himself had gone to Dakar to summon the Vichy French there to loyalty to the true France and to his own cause. They had disrespectfully opened up the battery of the harbor on him, and he had to come home. The clear indications were that the North African territory over which deGaulle felt he was entitled to exercise leadership would simply have fought him out.

Now Roosevelt having, as I say, only eight divisions with which to work, contemplated this North African campaign, and he did not intend to fight France in order to do that. His object was to fight General Rommel and the German and Italian armies who were then between the French-held territories and Egypt. It was in that respect that he made the pithy remark which was perhaps the greatest of his qualities. In crisis there was a certain cold, common sense which came out, as the arguments ebbed and flowed as to whether he should take the deGaulle leadership and follow the English line, or make his own. Having assessed, as I say, the deGaulle strike there, he said quite simply, "We are not going there to kill Frenchmen, so if you will, arrange this so that you don't have to do that." What that actually meant, of course, was trying to create a situation in North Africa in which the Vichy French armies who would not acknowledge deGaulle would also not fight the Anglo-American expeditionary forces but preferably ally with them.

We sent Robert Murphy there, not only as Consul General but really to make political preparations. You will find in Bob Murphy's book, *A Diplomat Among Warriors*, a very fair account of what he had to do. His immediate business was not to start a deGaullist revolution in North Africa. He was rather to mobilize and, if possible, to gain support of the French forces there even though they recognized Vichy, obeyed Marshall Pétain and that surprising and fantastic French admiral, [Jean] Darlan.

Now the end at least serves to evaluate the means, though it may not always justify it. The Rooseveltian policy worked. There was a little left-handed help from luck, a good deal of it as it happened. The North African expedition was launched [November 8, 1942]. Parenthetically, I may say that eight or 10 days during that period, I had some sleepless nights. In order to get this going, one of the things we had to assure ourselves of was that Spain would remain neutral at least until it got ashore. Spain was then in Franco's hands, and they had been dickering with the Germans. Some of us were asked to bet our lives' reputations and the safety of a vast expedition on our opinion that Spain would remain neutral, as it in fact did. The second battle of Guadalcanal was being fought in the Pacific at the same time, and if that battle had been lost and the expedition had failed, there was a very fair chance that before we got through we would be fighting this war off the San Francisco and New York harbors, instead of at the other side of the world. So I was, let us say, worried. Roosevelt was not. He said we had done everything we could do to make this work, and this is the soundest policy, and so here goes.

The North African expedition did succeed. As a result of it, a third of a whole continent came into Allied hands, and the total casualties were less than 300. [By the time the North African campaign ended in May 1943 allied casualties were on the order of 70,000, although the initial landing produced only light casualties.] This is less than the casualties, perhaps, in a single weekend of holiday-making here. You see, that for a wartime operation, this had probably saved more lives than it cost.

Then the fun began. The French troops in the immediate vicinity of it did not resist. They elected to abide events. This was the result of the Rooseveltian policy. In the interior there, French troops under General [Auguste] Nogues and others held out. They considered that the territory of France had been invaded by Americans and English, and they stated that they were going to resist and fight. They acknowledged orders from Admiral Darlan. Now Darlan — I will never know whether he intended it or not, I suspect he did because it is a French diplomatic trick — had been in Algiers at the time of the American landing. So he was captured by General Eisenhower and the landing forces. This may have been intentional on his part. After all, Tallyrand had done the same thing quite intentionally at the time of the close of the Napoleonic Wars, and I suppose Darlan was quite clever enough to have thought of that trick himself. A purely advantageous fact was that he had a son who had come down and was grievously ill with polio, also in Algiers. There was no hatred like the hatred between deGaulle's forces and Darlan and indeed, great numbers of French had considered that Darlan was a traitor — as to which they may have very well have been right.

Roosevelt was managing the situation day-to-day from the White House. Eden and Churchill believed that because Darlan was there (and we didn't immediately shoot him, I suppose) that his presence would wreck the underground political resistance in France and with it the Allied cause. Roosevelt received a wire from Eisenhower announcing that he had got this odd fish into his net. Roosevelt's first order was surprising. It said, "Get hold of Darlan and tell him that we would like to bring his son with polio to Warm Springs for treatment." This in the middle of war, and if I recall correctly, this was actually done. The second was to try to work out the end of the resistance of the French forces inland. What actually happened was that Darlan, finally convinced that he could do something or other with the American forces or at least had a better chance to do them with the American forces than otherwise, directed the rest of the French forces to end their resistance, which they thereupon did. [With the Allied invasion of North Africa, Germany had taken over the previously unoccupied part of France, until then controlled by the pro-German Vichy government. Rather than obey orders to resist, Admiral Darlan, the Vichy commander in North Africa, agreed to an armistice with the Allies which continued his control of French forces in Africa. The debate over the wisdom of U.S. cooperation with a Vichy official has never ended.] While everyone was still trying to figure out exactly what to do with Darlan, some of the deGaullist adherents in Algeria with typical directness assassinated him, and that was the end of the story. Meanwhile the nuts and bolts men had to go to work from one day to the next. Slowly they recreated a degree of unity in the French resistance. General deGaulle was brought there to work first with General [Henri] Geraud and establish his position if he could, which he did.

Roosevelt was quite as interested as the British in reconstituting France, a country he knew quite well and used to visit often. He had to bring the Vichy armies into North Africa somehow. He had to do it without a pitched battle. If that meant using the accident of capturing Darlan, he would use it and so instructed Eisenhower. And we know now — having, as we of course did not then, the German and Italian documents of the period, later captured after the war — that the success in North Africa ranks with the successful defense of Stalingrad as the turning point in the war as Mussolini clamored for more assistance from Hitler. Hitler, being unable to give it, engaged as he was on the Russian front, slowly came to quarrel with him. The net result, of course, was the defeat of Italy and the war back on European soil instead of beleaguering England and elsewhere.

Now, if you will see, that is the political engineer rather than the hero. These were not heroic poses that he was striking. This was dealing with things from day to day. But behind it was that passionate feeling that Americans were not in this war to kill Frenchmen. What we wanted at the end was some peace and friendship, not merely a victory by other means. This he succeeded in achieving.

That was a success, and I venture to speak of it because I had enough connection with it myself to be able to state that the facts are approximately as they seemed to men working on them, as they may today to historians. From this I want to draw my first conclusion. Roosevelt, I think, knew perfectly well that he was a historical figure. I don't think he ever considered himself a heroic figure, although he really did think people thought he was a heroic figure. Roosevelt was quite bright enough to know that. He was not competing with St. Peter in delivering judgments on men's souls, whether they were deGaulle or Darlan or anyone else. Instead, he was using men for what they were — their political possibilities, their immediate positions, their personal capacities — to move the whole program towards the greater objective which he could state with magnificent skill. Now in that he differed, I suppose, from more convinced moralists like President Woodrow Wilson, for whom I had worked, by the way, in the Versailles peace conference at the close of World War I. Not intimately, of course. The lowest advisor on the American delegation does not see very much of a president who is its presiding delegate. But enough at least so you could make a comparison of the two men's methods. Roosevelt discarded no one because he disliked him, or even because he disapproved of him. He wanted to make everyone useful. He reckoned at the same time that a man's usefulness, both at the time and in the future, might well be limited by the fact that man was a rascal or even a villain. He had plenty of experience with both. The question was not, therefore, what judgment to make of his character but what he could be used for at the moment. That judgment might be severely qualified by the fact that a rascal or a villain may not be dependable beyond a very tiny point. He took that into account. Having done that, he would hedge the bet as fully as he could and move steadily towards its objective and let St. Peter take care of the results.

Now my second illustration is more tragic. North Africa was a brilliant success. This was a failure. In 1945, France was on the way to being cleared or had wholly been cleared of the German troops after the Battle of the Bulge. The American and British armies were closing in on Germany. French troops, a French army mainly salvaged from North Africa, had been outfitted, financed, and transported by the United States to constitute a cross-Mediterranean invading force and General deGaulle had been placed at the head of it.

So they had decided on the Yalta Conference. The reason was that three armies would presently meet, a British, a French, and a Russian army in the middle of Europe. [An American army would, of course, also be involved.] It was thought that the time had come to talk this over and work out the situation, a perfectly tenable hypothesis. At the time I was Acting Under-Secretary of State, and I have been opposed to this move. Perhaps I was opposed to it because one of my jobs was liaison with the intelligence service at that time, and I was pretty clear that the Soviet Union had lost interest in cooperating with British and Americans, probably also with the French. The action of American troops against Germany from there on was not likely to affect their fate. In fact, they were almost in the situation to handle Hitler themselves from the eastern front. So they had very little further interest in us, quite irrespective of the alliance or the declaration by the United Nations and so forth.

Stalin was now playing the Soviet hand against the field, and the Soviet Union intended at that time, if it could, to dominate all of continental Europe. I think there is no possible doubt if you read the documents. For that purpose her people were using the Communist-organized underground movements everywhere, all the way from Warsaw to Paris. Then as now, the undergrounds were partly merely nationalists and in part dominated by small and active groups of Communist organizers. They were perhaps the ablest organizers in Europe at that time.

The Russians had already pushed their armies beyond the

pre-war Russian frontiers, and increasingly it was plain to some of us, or at least I thought, that wherever the Russian armies stood, there the Russian power and the communist organization would stay. Specifically, they were seizing Poland. They were constituting a Polish government. They were making it, for the time being at least, a captive of Russia, as most of Poland had been for more than a century before World War I. I thought that the Yalta Conference and its underlying motive, the necessity for redeploying American troops in Europe to finish the war in Japan as soon as the armistice came, would lead to trouble. Better let events take their course.

It was partly because of that that I left my assistant secretaryship and asked to be sent to the field and went, in point of fact, as ambassador to Brazil. And as it happened, I returned to Washington just after President Roosevelt had returned from the Yalta Conference. I went to see him. You are aware of what the Yalta Conference did. It turned over Poland, whose independence had been guaranteed by Britain and by all of us, to Russian occupation from which it could only emerge by a long historical process, as it will. But it will be a long time. This is not to mention a great many other things which we needn't go into here. [The advancing Red Army had already occupied Poland by the time of the Yalta Conference, February 4-11, 1945. FDR and Churchill extracted from Stalin a general pledge that the communist-dominated Lublin government would be reorganized to include other elements and that free elections would be held in the near future. The Yalta Conference also considered the post-war status of Germany, the creation of the United Nations, and the war against Japan, all of which Roosevelt regarded as more uncertain and critical.]

The Yalta Conference had done this: taken in return for an actual acceptance of a territorial position, a lot of words which might or might not mean anything. And I was very, very unhappy. I came into the president's office, and he didn't wait. He put up both arms and he said, "Adolf, I didn't say the result was good. I said it was the best I could do." And he was tired and spent. I put my arm around him and tried to make laughter and failed. He wanted to talk. I may add that for those of you who are inexperienced in the matter, presidents don't have to explain themselves to assistant secretaries or to ambassadors or indeed to anyone else, except that it is wise for him to explain himself to his Secretary of State and to his cabinet officers. But he wanted to do that. But then we had been friends since before he had become president, and we were in the habit of talking with a frankness which I cherish even now. He said, "I said it was the best I could do." And he wanted to talk. Then he explained patiently. He said he had gotten the Russian word for reconstituting of the countries under Russian occupation. There were to be free elections and government freely chosen. They were thus to choose their own regimes. He knew this was only an agreement and in international affairs, agreements are not always kept. But, as he said, the chiefs of staff were pushing the need to take American forces out of Europe and to deploy them against Japan, and since we could not push troops into the area without pressure behind, we had to rely on the Russian word. The chiefs also wanted Russian participation against Japan in their final drive as the Japanese war, which then was not ended, closed. By the way, the nuclear bomb was not then in existence. He was explaining why he had done what he had done and concluded by saying again, "I told you that was the best I could do. I don't think it's good."

Now I thought, and President Roosevelt knew it because we had corresponded about it, that the Russians would not be much help against Japan. I thought the Japanese were even then seeking ways and means to end the war, and no particular sacrifices needed to be made to assure the cooperation of Stalin. But the president knew, and so unhappily did I, that assistant secretaries of state, especially in wartime, don't override the cold calculations of the military chiefs. The military chiefs in any event are responsible for results, not to say, the lives of hundreds of thousands of Americans under their command. If it was a question of what I thought or what they thought, I didn't really have any chance, and I knew that, so did he.

But even then Roosevelt was mulling over the methods, persuasions, and pressures by which the Soviet Union might be induced to keep their word, taking seriously the obligation we had to those countries which we would call today the iron curtain countries. But also, he was steering toward the greater objective. If the Soviet Union, the United States, and Great Britain, together with the countries emerging from Nazi occupation, could cooperate in victory as well as in war, we might have a glorious, peaceful reconstruction, something that rarely occurs in history. He had forseen and was endeavoring to forestall what in day-to-day language we call the Cold War and which has plagued the world for 20 years and rises even now to the boiling point in Southeast Asia. So combining the necessities of one situation with the hopes of the other, he had thrown this out and endeavored to maintain this as a steady and consistent ideal. He thought that the Russians had no longer a need to be afraid. Because of that, positions could be asserted. He was considering how to use his own influence — which was enormous — to bring this about.

Now you will see that so far as history is concerned, Yalta has to be accounted a failure. I mean by that, that whatever the men meeting there intended, they did not intend what happened. They certainly did not intend the Cold War. They did not intend to whet the Communist imperialist appetites by the concessions they then made, and they did not intend to have an undercover struggle — not always undercover either — for great parts of the world, let alone to lay the outlines of a third World War. So one could believe just at I did that there was no chance of having any favorable result at Yalta, as I did before the conference itself. One could be unhappy about the results of that conference and at the same time one could, as I did, fervently hope that the attempt they were making just might be successful. For had it been successful, of course, hundreds of thousands of men now dead would have lived, and the state of the world would be infinitely happier than it is today. Failure though it was, the Yalta Conference was the failure of a very big man, apprehending and seeking to prevent precisely the perilous and painful course of events in which we are still entangled.

Now no one can prove an historical might-have-been. Consequently it can never be known whether success at Yalta was at all possible. What we did have was a military problem which appeared to call for transfer of American forces away from Europe to the Pacific. We did have the known problem that the probability was that the Soviet Union would take advantage of that redeployment to seize the mid-European countries or part of them, and particularly Poland which beyond all deserved reconstitution and peace. Unable to meet that situation with force because we needed the force on the other side of the world and fearing also the effects of force in that region, Roosevelt attempted to fill the gap by Stalin's word, relying in part on

Roosevelt's own heroic world position to keep that word valid. He was in fact proposing to use his hero position, then towering in Europe, as an asset. He had no illusion that the myth was the reality. He was prepared to use the myth of himself as an instrument in that situation if it could be useful to assume that the Yalta accords would be kept. As a factual matter, at the time of his death, with the very last of his ebbing strength, he was studying how best he could do it.

So I draw a second conclusion. I suggest a new dimension in a famous conflict of ideas. All of us have been brought up on the antithesis between Carlyle and Tolstoy. Carlyle's classic essay, "Heroes and Hero Worshipers," suggests that history is made by men of heroic stature who control events. Tolstoy, in *War and Peace*, of course asserts that men, no matter now heroic their image, are invariably unwitting instruments of social historical forces whose direction, impact and results they cannot change because they are used by them and cannot use them. Now I suggest just possibly that the heroic position that one attains in his lifetime may itself be used as a historical force. It may even be used by the man himself. But to be able to do that the man has to be able to distinguish the mythological hero image prevailing outside his palace, his office, or his White House from his own historical self. Equally, he has to be able to appreciate the external possibilities of that heroic personality. I think Roosevelt did both. This involved a detachment so great that he never mistook the hero position as an accurate portrait of himself. Rather he would laugh. Still less did the detachment permit him to ignore the possible usefulness of his heroic position as a tool. It would have been silly to describe the asset. Roosevelt had the detachment and as a super-politician was content to use his own hero legend, especially if, as was true at the time the Yalta Conference ended, he probably had no effective tool.

His death in April 1945 ended the tale, for that is the limitation of the hero myth, the heroic image as a tool, and the life itself. All of them, after all, depend on the life of a man, and Roosevelt was no more immortal than anyone else. All of them end with that life. They end, that is to say, in the areas of action not carried forward by an institution's surviving the individual and endeavoring to perpetuate the individual's ideas, objectives, dreams. That is the precise difference between the surviving influence of Roosevelt in the United States and perhaps the fading influence of Roosevelt elsewhere. You see, in America, the man and the myth and the man using the myth were all translated into ongoing institutions which the younger of you take for granted but which were unheard of when I first entered the government in 1933. They were translated into ongoing institutions and grafted into that continuing current which is the constitutional, historical government and political structure of the United States.

Unquestionably, his greatest domestic achievement was the enlargement of the responsibility of the federal government, whether you like it or not. I personally think that it was essential. Roosevelt in the Congress of the Hundred Days had caused our government to assume responsibility for the economic and social functioning of the country, a task the federal government had never assumed before. No one will ever reverse that conception of the task of the White House, the Congress, and the men in Washington. In increasing measure, that conception, carried out during his lifetime, is being carried out and developed even today. And that was Roosevelt in his own country, channeling its political forces, shaping its laws, educating its people, bringing them to assume twentieth century responsibilities in twentieth century conditions and by twentieth century methods. Meanwhile the heroic image gradually fades. The historical man increasingly emerges. The reality closes the myth, but the conception Roosevelt had no longer needs the myth.

Crowds watch Franklin D. Roosevelt funeral procession in Washington D.C., April 1, 1945. [Office of War Information photo, National Archives]

CHAPTER TWELVE

FDR's America

The Roosevelt era produced many significant changes in the government and society of the United States. Most noticeable was the reshaping of the Presidency. The growth of presidential power to the point where the chief executive enjoyed virtual supremacy in the federal government — what some historians have come to label "The Imperial Presidency" clearly had deep roots in the Roosevelt administration. Dissatisfied with the reserved style of his predecessor, FDR, in the 30s, was continually proposing new federal programs, appealing to various groups for support, seeking to bend Congress to his will, and publicly explaining his actions. The White House dominated the legislative process to a degree never before known. Furthermore, by frequent press conferences, radio broadcasts, and nationwide travel, FDR established an image of involvement, of direct presidential contact with the people and their problems. Even those who detested Roosevelt did not doubt his responsibility for what transpired. Liberals and others, unhappy with the seeming inaction of Congress and President Hoover, were delighted at the vigor Roosevelt displayed in attacking the depression. They argued that the problems of modern society required the forceful leadership of a powerful and active chief executive.

The growing importance of foreign affairs further enhanced the Presidency. The apparent wisdom of FDR's policies to aid Britain and prepare the U.S. for war, as well as the poor judgment of congressional isolationists, led many to conclude in retrospect that presidents were better equipped than Congress to understand and manage foreign policy. The war did even more to expand presidential power. The military need for secrecy and quick decision and the constitutional latitude given a wartime president allowed Roosevelt to act without consulting Congress or the people. Among other things, commitments were made to allies, and the atomic bomb (which would end the war in the Pacific without a costly invasion of Japan) was developed in total secrecy. The successful conclusion of the war made Roosevelt's decisions once again look astute and reinforced arguments for a strong Presidency. Several succeeding administrations would contribute to the rise of an "Imperial Presidency," but each built upon foundations erected between 1933 and 1945.

The New Deal and World War II altered the federal government's role in American life. Before 1933, individual citizens generally encountered the federal government only when they used the mails, paid their annual income tax bill, or entered the military service (itself a fairly rare occurrence). The reforms of the 1930s brought the federal government in direct contact with the farmer (who was aided by production restrictions, price supports, and rural electrification), the worker (whose union elections and bargaining rights were supervised and insured), the unemployed (who found jobs with the CCC or WPA), the young (two million of whom held part-time jobs created by the National Youth Administration), and the aged (for whom Social Security benefits were often the major source of income). Not everyone benefitted from New Deal programs, but for the millions who did, the federal government became a more immediate part of their lives. During World War II, the return of prosperity and the preoccupation of the government with other matters prompted abandonment of many New Deal relief agencies, among them the CCC, WPA, and NYA. Yet the federal government touched individual lives even more during the war as agencies rationed goods, regulated wages and prices, withheld taxes from every paycheck, and determined whether one would work in a defense plant at home or go to war. As the roles of state and local governments declined, it became common to refer to the federal government as "the government."

The relationship also changed between the federal government and American business. With few exceptions, business operated free of government regulation before the New Deal. Indeed a main thrust of government activity in the 1920s had been to aid expansion of free enterprise at home and abroad. The Roosevelt administration did not try to revolutionize the economy. On the contrary, it repeatedly sought to save capitalism. American business was overseen and regulated so as not to destroy itself through excesses and so that the public would regain confidence in banks, stock exchanges, and the economic future. By making government an employer of last resort and a stimulator of a depressed economy, the New Deal secured the foundation of the capitalistic system without destroying its central feature: private economic decision-making for private gain. World War II, for all its government regulation, entrusted production and distribution to private hands, provided American business a handsome profit, and in its wake, left a private enterprise economy restored to prosperity and dominated more than ever before by large corporations. Far from destroying capitalism, the Roosevelt administration, through supervision and assistance, saved it from collapse and ushered a new age of unparalleled growth.

American society adopted a new appearance between 1933 and 1945, while retaining much of the old and familiar. Farmers, workers, and businessmen, not to mention blacks and women, found their lives changed somewhat. The welfare state approach of the Roosevelt administration reduced the destitution of the depression and provided certain guarantees against failure to individuals and businesses, while leaving most social and economic decisions in private hands.

When war came, labor shortages replaced the high unemployment of the 1930s, doubling the average family income between 1939 and 1945. The success of the OPA in checking inflation made this a real gain. New higher income tax rates, especially on large incomes, reduced the share of national income received by the wealthiest. (The highest-paid five percent of the population received about 25 percent of all income in 1940, but their share fell to 18 percent by 1945.) The principal beneficiary was the middle class whose tendency to spend the increased income fueled the prosperous, high-consumption postwar decades. Those on the bottom rungs of the economic ladder increased their actual dollar earnings, but their proportion of total income, relative to the middle and upper classes, improved very little. The strengthening of the middle class at the expense of the upper class, leaving the lower class undisturbed, accelerated a shift which began in the 1930s and established an income distribution pattern in America which has changed little since the 1940s.

The prosperity of wartime encouraged childbearing. In the depressed 30s, few felt they could afford a family; the yearly population increase of .73 percent was, up to that time, the lowest in American history. During the war attitudes changed, and the annual increase reached 1.20 percent. The post-war optimism and prosperity brought a "baby boom," a growth rate of 1.72 percent in the late 1940s and 1.85 percent in the 50s. These fluctuations in the birth rate would mean a lifetime of opportunity for the generation born in the 1930s and a constant overcrowding in school, in the job market, and elsewhere for the baby-boom generation.

The war prompted tremendous population shifts. Military service forced millions to move temporarily. But perhaps most striking was the more permanent migration of persons into areas where war industries developed. Five and one half million people left the farm for the city. A million southerners, many of them black, moved north. Nowhere was growth stimulated as much as on the west coast. Cities such as Portland, Seattle, Los Angeles, and San Francisco boomed with aircraft and shipbuilding contracts and military installations. The population of California jumped by 20 percent during the war. Not only did the war cause increased urbanization and a westward shift of population, but it also helped homogenize the American people; the result of so many workers, soldiers, and dependents traveling to distant parts of the country, experiencing new social customs, and learning to behave in standard ways.

As a result of the 1930s and especially the war, American society became more mobile, more urban, more industrial, more homogeneous. In growing numbers, Americans worked for big business or big government, belonged to big unions, and lived in big cities. These social changes made the lives of Americans more alike, but also made individuals more anonymous and rootless. The community in which each individual had an identity, a recognized function, and a sense of belonging was becoming a thing of the past. The frustrations of life in an impersonal mass society, a growing social problem during the Roosevelt years, remain unresolved today.

The years of the Roosevelt Presidency were crucial in the development of modern America. The accounts included in this book touch on some important issues which students of the New Deal and World War II should consider. Was the emergence of a stronger Presidency a necessary or wise response to the crises of depression and war? James Farley, Rexford Tugwell, and Adolf Berle seem to believe so. Jouett Shouse vigorously disagrees. Did the federal government effectively respond to the problems of the day? Milo Reno, Rex Murray, Elmer Powers, Walter White, Fulton Lewis, Jr., and FDR himself, offer differing views. Did either the New Deal or World War II radically reshape American society? If so, how? If not, why not? Various suggestions are to be found in the accounts of Shouse, Murray, Powers, White, the seven Louisianans, Mary Anderson, Margaret Hickey, and Mary Elizabeth Pidgeon. Undoubtedly, the reader of these first-hand accounts will have many other questions. Not all of the questions surrounding the era can be answered, certainly not from the few accounts presented here. But by considering the issues and some of the viewpoints which have been put forth, one can begin to better understand the legacy of FDR's America.

Suggestions for Further Reading

A great deal has been written about the New Deal and World War II. This short, selective list concentrates on books readily available in paperback editions and in most college or public libraries. (Paperbacks are noted by an asterisk.) Someone interested in more extensive and specialized bibliographies should consult William H. Cartwright and Richard L. Watson, Jr., eds., *The Reinterpretation of American History and Culture* (Washington, 1973) and William J. Stewart, *The Era of Franklin D. Roosevelt: A Selected Bibliography of Periodical, Essay, and Dissertation Literature, 1945-1971* (Hyde Park, 1974) as well as bibliographies in the books listed below.

First-hand accounts of the Roosevelt administration are plentiful. James A. Farley's account of FDR's first two elections, *Behind the Ballots* (New York, 1938) was followed by a rather bitter account of his dispute with Roosevelt in 1940, *Jim Farley's Story: The Roosevelt Years* (New York, 1948). Rexford Tugwell provided an excellent, generally sympathetic study of the New Deal and its leader, *The Democratic Roosevelt* (New York, 1957),* and an account of the 1932 campaign, *The Brains Trust* (New York, 1968).* Adolf Berle's memoirs were published after his death as Beatrice Bishop Berle and Travis Beale Jacobs, eds., *Navigating the Rapids 1918-1971: From the Papers of Adolf A. Berle* (New York, 1973). Other interesting memoirs are Eleanor Roosevelt, *This I Remember* (New York, 1949), Frances Perkins, *The Roosevelt I Knew* (New York, 1946)*, Raymond Moley, *After Seven Years* (New York, 1939)* and *The First New Deal* (New York, 1966), Harold L. Ickes, *The Secret Diary of Harold L. Ickes* (3 vols.; New York, 1953-1954), John Morton Blum, *Roosevelt and Morgenthau* (Boston, 1970)*, and, for the war years in particular, Robert E. Sherwood, *Roosevelt and Hopkins: An Intimate History* (New York, 1950)*.

The depression and its impact on American society have been examined in various ways. Vivid personal testimony is found in David Shannon, ed., *The Great Depression* (Englewood Cliffs, 1960)*, Rita J. Simon, ed., *As We Saw the Thirties* (Urbana, 1967)*, and Studs Terkel, *Hard Times: An Oral History of the Great Depression* (New York, 1970)*. Robert and Helen Lynd, *Middletown in Transition* (New York, 1937)* is a valuable, detailed study of one city. There is fascinating detail in Edward Robb Ellis, *A Nation in Torment: The Great American Depression, 1929-1939* (New York, 1970)*. An outstanding novel, offering a realistic account of depression misery and frustration is John Steinbeck, *The Grapes of Wrath* (New York, 1939)*.

Some of the best general studies of the period focus on Franklin Roosevelt. Particularly insightful and well written are two volumes by James MacGregor Burns, *Roosevelt: The Lion and the Fox* (New York, 1956)*, which concentrates on the 30s, and *Roosevelt: The Soldier of Freedom* (New York, 1970)*, dealing with the war years. Kenneth S. Davis, *FDR: The Beckoning of Destiny, 1882-1928* (New York, 1972)* effectively covers that span. The other two major biographies of FDR are incomplete. Frank Freidel, *Franklin D. Roosevelt* (4 vols.; Boston, 1952-1973; only volume 4, *Launching the New Deal*, is in paper) carries the story through the summer of 1933, and Arthur Schlesinger, Jr., *The Age of Roosevelt* (3 vols.; Boston, 1957-60)* through the election of 1936. Joseph P. Lash provides a different perspective in *Eleanor and Franklin* (New York, 1971)*. Still the best one-volume survey is William E. Leuchtenburg, *Franklin D. Roosevelt and the New Deal, 1932-1940* (New York, 1963)*. An excellent brief analysis is Paul K. Conkin, *FDR and the Origins of the Welfare State* (New York, 1967), published in paperback as *The New Deal.*

The New Deal legislative program has been studied in great detail. A particularly useful analysis of the often contradictory economic policies of the Roosevelt administration is Ellis W. Hawley, *The New Deal and the Problem of Monopoly* (Princeton, 1966)*. Also helpful for a general understanding of legislative developments are Bernard Sternsher, *Rexford Tugwell and the New Deal* (New Brunswick, N.J., 1964), J. Joseph Huthmacher, *Senator Robert F. Wagner and the Rise of Urban Liberalism* (New York, 1968)* and James T. Patterson,

Congressional Conservatism and the New Deal (Lexington, 1967)*. More specialized are Bernard Bellush, *The Failure of the NRA* (New York, 1975)*; John A. Salmond, *The Civilian Conservative Corps, 1933-1942* (Durham, 1967); Daniel Nelson, *Unemployment Insurance: The American Experience, 1915-1935* (Madison, 1969); Paul K. Conkin, *Tomorrow a New World: The New Deal Community Program* (Ithaca, 1959); and William F. McDonald, *Federal Relief Administration and the Arts* (Columbus, 1969). Barry D. Karl, *Executive Reorganization and Reform in the New Deal* (Cambridge, 1963) has broader significance than its title implies, as does James T. Patterson, *The New Deal and the States: Federalism in Transition* (Princeton, 1969). The impact of the New Deal on one section is examined briefly in Frank Friedel, *F.D.R. and the South* (Baton Rouge, 1965)* and in detail in George B. Tindall, *The Emergence of the New South, 1913-1945* (Baton Rouge, 1967)*.

Agriculture in the 30s has been examined from several perspectives. Farm policies of the New Deal are considered in Christiana M. Campbell, *The Farm Bureau and the New Deal* (Urbana, 1962), Van L. Perkins, *Crisis in Agriculture: The Agriculture Adjustment Administration and the New Deal, 1933* (Berkeley, 1969), and Richard S. Kirkendall, *Social Scientists and Farm Politics in the Age of Roosevelt* (Columbia, 1966). FDR's Secretary of Agriculture is the subject of Edward L. and Frederick H. Schapsmeier, *Henry A. Wallace of Iowa: The Agrarian Years, 1910-1940* (Ames, 1968). Agrarian protest is studied in Theodore Saloutos and John D. Hicks, *Agrarian Discontent in the Middle West, 1900-1939 (Madison, 1951)*, John L. Shover, *Cornbelt Rebellion: The Farmers' Holiday Association* (Urbana, 1965), and Donald H. Grubbs, *Cry from the Cotton: The Southern Tenant Farmers' Union and the New Deal* (Chapel Hill, 1971). In 1975 Arno Press reprinted Roland A. White, *Milo Reno: Farmers Union Pioneer* (Iowa City, 1941). More of Elmer Powers's view of Iowa in the depression can be found in H. Roger Grant and L. Edward Purcell, *Years of Struggle: The Farm Diary of Elmer G. Powers, 1931-1936* (Ames, 1976).

The study of workers during the 30s has, for the most part, been the investigation of union organizing. Irving Bernstein, *Turbulent Years: A History of the American Worker, 1933-1941* (Boston, 1969)*, well written and excellent, pays considerable attention to the rise of the CIO, while the standard work on the opposition is Philip Taft, *The A.F. of L. from the Death of Gompers to the Merger* (New York, 1959). Two studies of congressional involvement with unionism are the previously-mentioned Huthmacher biography of Robert Wagner and Jerold Auerbach, *Labor and Liberty: The LaFollette Committee and the New Deal* (Indianapolis, 1966). A crucial labor-management dispute is examined in Sidney Fine, *Sit-Down: The General Motors Strike of 1936-1937* (Ann Arbor, 1967). Milton Derber and Edwin Young, eds., *Labor and the New Deal* (Madison, 1957) brings together much useful material.

Critics of the New Deal have seldom received favorable treatment from historians, but at least they have not been overlooked. Goerge Wolfskill and John A. Hudson survey the opposition in *All but the People: Franklin D. Roosevelt and His Critics, 1933-1939* (New York, 1969) while Wolfskill looks at the American Liberty League in *The Revolt of the Conservatives* (Boston, 1962). Donald R. McCoy examines the left in *Angry Voices: Left-of-Center Politics in the New Deal Era* (Lawrence, 1958) and FDR's 1936 Republican opponent in *Landon of Kansas* (Lincoln, 1966). Perhaps the best biography of any figure from the 30s is T. Harry Williams, *Huey Long* (New York, 1969)*. Also useful are Morton Keller, *In Defense of Yesterday: James Beck and the Politics of Conservatism, 1861-1936* (New York, 1958), David H. Bennett, *Demagogues in the Depression: American Radicals and the Union Party, 1932-1936* (New Brunswick, 1969), and Charles J. Tull, *Father Coughlin and the New Deal* (Syracuse, 1965).

The black experience is surveyed in Raymond Wolters, *Negroes and the Great Depression* (Westport, 1970)*, Bernard Sternsher, ed., *The Negro in Depression and War: Prelude to Revolution, 1930-1945* (Chicago, 1969)*, and a classic contemporary study, Gunnar Myrdal, *An American Dilemma* (2 vols., New York, 1944)*. The memories of two NAACP leaders are recorded in Mary White Ovington, *The Walls Came Tumbling Down* (New York, 1947)* and Walter F. White, *A Man Called White* (New York, 1948)*. A celebrated 30s rape case which had racial overtones is described in Dan T. Carter, *Scottsboro: A Tragedy of the American South* (Baton Rouge, 1969)*. Black progress during World War II is measured in Herbert Garfinkel, *When Negroes March: The March on Washington Movement in the Organizational Politics for FEPC* (Glencoe, 1951)*, Jervis

Anderson, *A. Philip Randolph* (New York, 1973)*, and Richard
M. Dalfiume, *Desegregation of the U.S. Armed Forces: Fighting
on Two Fronts, 1939-1953* (Columbia, 1969).

Not surprisingly, no other single aspect of the Roosevelt
administration has received as much attention as the conduct of
foreign affairs. Economic diplomacy during the 30s is the subject
of Herbert Feis, *1933: Characters in Crisis* (Boston, 1966)* and,
from a much different viewpoint, Lloyd C. Gardner, *Economic
Aspects of New Deal Diplomacy* (Madison, 1964)*. Among the
best of the many discussions of American attempts to avoid war
and the various steps which led to war are Robert A. Divine, *The
Illusion of Neutrality* (Chicago, 1962)*, William Langer and S.
Everett Gleason, *The Challenge to Isolation* (2 vols.; New York,
1952)* and *The Undeclared War* (New York, 1953), Herbert Feis,
The Road to Pearl Harbor (Princeton, 1950)*, Warren F.
Kimball, *The Most Unsordid Act: Lend-Lease, 1939-1941*
(Baltimore, 1969), and Roberta Wohlstetter, *Pearl Harbor:
Warning and Decision* (Stanford, 1962)*.

The domestic side of World War II has not received nearly
the attention it deserves. There are, nevertheless, some excellent
books available. Richard Polenberg, *War and Society: The United
States, 1941-1945* (Philadelphia, 1972)* and Geoffrey Perrett,
*Days of Sadness, Years of Triumph: The American People,
1939-1945* (Baltimore, 1973)* describe and measure the impact
of war. Additional information on the society during war can be
found in Richard R. Lingeman, *Don't You Know There's A War
On? The American Home Front, 1941-1945* (Englewood Cliffs,
1973)* and Richard Polenberg, *America at War: The Home
Front, 1941-1945* (Englewood Cliffs, 1968)*. The most notori-
ous instance of wartime suppression of civil liberties is described
in Roger A. Daniels, *Concentration Camps USA: Japanese-
Americans and World War II* (New York, 1971)*. Donald Nelson,
Arsenal of Democracy: The Story of American War Production
(New York, 1946) offers the War Production Board administra-
tor's view of government economic regulation. Two helpful
accounts of the rubber crisis are Frank A. Howard's one-sided
Buna Rubber: The Birth of an Industry (New York, 1947) and
Robert A. Solo's harder-to-find *Synthetic Rubber: A Case Study
in Technological Development Under Government Direction*,
Study 18 of the Subcommittee on Patents, Trademarks, and

Copyrights of the Committee on the Judiciary (Washington, 1959). Fulton Lewis, Jr., is described in a different context in David H. Culbert, *News for Everyman: Radio Commentators and Foreign Affairs in Thirties America* (Westport, 1976).

Women have not received much attention as a group, either during the 1930s or the war. Outstanding individuals fared the best. Eleanor Roosevelt and Francis Perkins produced memoirs, and the first lady was examined in Lash's *Eleanor and Franklin*, all noted above. Less well-known is *Woman at Work: The Autobiography of Mary Anderson as told to Mary N. Winslow* (Minneapolis, 1951). The impact of World War II provides the focus of an excellent survey by William Chafe, *The American Woman: Her Changing Social, Economic and Political Roles, 1920-1970* (New York, 1972)*. Useful studies of women war workers include Caroline Bird, *Born Female* (New York, 1968)*, Alva Myrdal and Viola Klein, *Women's Two Roles: Home and Work* (London, 1956)*, Elizabeth Baker, *Technology and Women's Work* (New York, 1964), Valerie Oppenheimer, *The Female Labor Force in the United States* (Berkeley, 1970), and Augusta Clawson, *Shipyard Diary of a Woman Welder* (London, 1944).

The military history of World War II has been examined almost as intensively as that of the Civil War. For anyone interested in battles, campaigns, or generals, a lifetime of reading awaits in multi-volume government-sponsored histories as well as commercial publications. For an overview of American military policy, a good starting point is Walter Millis, *Arms and Men* (New York, 1956)*. A. Russell Buchanan, *The United States and World War II* (2 vols.; New York, 1964)* is a good survey. Barbara Tuchman, *Stillwell and the American Experience in China, 1941-1945* (New York, 1971)* deals with one often-overlooked phase of the war in a very interesting fashion and has much broader implications than its title suggests. For the experience of the relatively few Americans who actually saw combat, Norman Mailer's first novel, *The Naked and the Dead* (New York, 1948)*, is superb.

Wartime diplomacy and preparations for the war's end are well treated in Burns, *The Soldier of Freedom*, mentioned earlier, as well as Robert A. Divine's brief *Roosevelt and World War II* (Baltimore, 1969)*. Divine's *Second Chance: The Triumph of*

Internationalism in America during World War II (New York, 1967)* tells the story of the formation of the United Nations. The wartime roots of postwar difficulties are exposed in Diane Shaver Clemens, *Yalta* (New York, 1970)* and John Lewis Gaddis, *The United States and the Origins of the Cold War, 1941-1947* (New York, 1972)*.